My Life in Jesus

Illustrated by Ed Koehler

CPH®

SAINT LOUIS

What is the Small Catechism?

The Small Catechism is a book of instruction, in the form of questions and answers, that sums up the teachings of the Bible. It divides the truths of God's Word into Six Chief Parts:

The Ten Commandments
The Creed
The Lord's Prayer
The Sacrament of Holy Baptism
Confession
The Sacrament of the Altar

Who wrote our Small Catechism?

Martin Luther, the Reformer of the church, wrote the Small Catechism in 1529.

Why are the Six Chief Parts of the Small Catechism taken from the Bible alone?

All the chief parts of the Small Catechism are taken from the Bible, because as God's written Word the Bible is the only final authority for Christian faith and life.

What is the key to the correct understanding of the Bible?

Jesus Christ, the Savior of the world, is the heart and center of the Scripture and therefore the key to its true meaning.

Life Point

God gives us eternal life through faith in Jesus, the Savior. The Small Catechism is a guidebook that helps us understand this and the other important truths of God's Word on which our Christian faith and life are based.

MY LIFE IN JESUS STUDENT LEAFLETS are published by Concordia Publishing House, 3558 S. Jefferson Ave., St. Louis, MO 63118-3968. Skit scripts written by Diane Grebing. Edited by Edward Grube. Scripture quotations: NIV®. Used by permission of Zondervan. All rights reserved. Catechism quotations: *Luther's Small Catechism with Explanation,* © 1986, 1991 CPH. Copyright © 2000 CPH. Printed in U.S.A.

22-2874

God has given us eternal life, and this life is in His Son.
1 John 5:11

Camp counselor ABBY stands with ALEX, SEAN, T. J., STEPHANIE, and KARA near the Camp Wonderment entrance. The students' backpacks, duffle bags, sleeping bags, and other gear are stashed around them at their feet. JESS stands well away from the others with her back turned toward them. She angrily crosses her arms.

Getting Acquainted

ABBY: (Cheerfully, with clipboard in hand, hammer hanging out of her pocket) Welcome to Camp Wonderment! My name is Abby, and I'm your counselor for the next two weeks. For many of you, this camp is a new experience. I'm here as your friend to guide and help you. I hope we'll have a great time together. First, I need to find out who each of you is. (Looks down at clipboard) Is there an Alex in this group?

ALEX: (Cautiously raising his hand) I'm Alex.

ABBY: (Extends hand in greeting) Good to meet you, Alex. I noticed on your camp application that you have lots of talent with arts and crafts.

ALEX: Yeah, I drew the logo for our school shirts this year and helped with the silk screening.

ABBY: Neat! Every year during the second week of camp we design some camp shirts. I'd appreciate your expertise. (Looks down at clipboard, then searches group) Which one of you is Stephanie?

STEPHANIE: (Steps forward) That's me!

ABBY: I see from my list, Stephanie, that you were one of last year's campers. I'm glad you're back. (Turns to KARA) Kara, right?

KARA: (Moves slowly toward ABBY with the help of a crutch) Yes. I'm sorry it takes me so long to move. Until my knee heals from surgery, the doctor says I have use this thing. (Wiggles crutch)

ABBY: (Kindly) I'll do all I can for you, Kara. (Winks) You know, that crutch might come in handy as a snake club!

STEPHANIE: (Squeamishly) There are snakes here?

ABBY: (Laughs) Only the rubber kind a joker might hide in your sleeping bag!

T. J. and SEAN step toward ABBY. A yo-yo hangs out of SEAN's pocket.

T. J.: I'm T. J. (Points his thumb toward SEAN) This is Sean. Where's the lake? I'm ready to swim!

ABBY: Hang on for a little while, T. J. We'll have plenty of time for swimming later. (Looks at SEAN's pocket) Hey, Sean! Is that a yo-yo I see?

SEAN shyly smiles and nods yes.

T. J.: Sean's a yo-yo whiz. Whenever I try it, I just knot up the string.

ABBY: Maybe you can teach us some yo-yo tricks sometime, Sean.

SEAN smiles and nods.

KARA: Do you know what cabin I'm in?

ABBY: Sure do! The boys are in number 5 down by the mess hall. You, me, Stephanie, and Jess are in number 7 up on the hill. (Looks around curiously) I wonder where Jess is.

ALEX: (Gesturing behind him) I think that's her over there. (Whispering to ABBY) I've seen her around my school. She likes to cause trouble.

ABBY: (Walks confidently over to JESS) Hi. Are you Jess?

JESS: (Turns toward ABBY with a cross look) Maybe. Who wants to know?

ABBY: I do. I'm Abby. As I look at my list of campers, you're on it. Welcome to Camp Wonderment.

JESS: (Looks around with a sneer) I wonder what I'm doing here. I can't believe I have to spend two weeks in this place.

ABBY: I think you'll find this place a lot of fun once you meet the other campers and learn your way around.

JESS: (Gesturing at the other campers) The less time I have to spend with those geeks the better.

ABBY: (Patiently) Jess, here at camp we respect each other. That respect includes not calling each other names. (Pauses briefly) Let's go join the others. I've got some things I need to share with everyone.

ABBY strides back to the group, hammer and flyer from her clipboard in hand. JESS reluctantly picks up her backpack and shuffles over to the tree. She stands a short distance away from the others.

ABBY: Before I show you where you can stow your gear, I want to begin by telling you some important information.

ABBY turns and begins to hammer a piece of paper titled "Camp Wonderment Rules" to the tree.

JESS: (Disgustedly) Oh, man! Rules! This camp is just like the rest!

My Life in Jesus

How do you feel when you're at a place for the first time?

What are some helpful things to know whenever you begin something new?

As a Christian, on what can you depend no matter where you find yourself in life?

What are the Ten Commandments?

The Ten Commandments are the Law of God.

What is the summary of all the commandments?

Love is the summary of all the commandments. As Jesus explained, this love includes love for God and love for your neighbor (Matthew 22:37, 39).

The First Commandment

You shall have no other gods.

What does this mean? We should fear, love, and trust in God above all things.

Who is the only true God?

The only true God is the triune God: Father, Son, and Holy Spirit, three distinct persons in one divine being (the Holy Trinity).

What does God forbid in the First Commandment?

God forbids us to have other gods (idolatry).

How do we fear, love, and trust in God above all things?

We **fear** God above all things when we revere Him alone as the highest being, honor Him with our lives, and avoid what displeases Him. We **love** God above all things when we cling to Him alone as our God and gladly devote our lives to His service. We **trust** in God above all things when we commit our lives completely to His keeping and rely on Him for help in every need.

Life Point

We worship God alone as we live under His love and goodness.

MY LIFE IN JESUS STUDENT LEAFLETS are published by Concordia Publishing House, 3558 S. Jefferson Ave., St. Louis, MO 63118-3968. Skit scripts written by Diane Grebing. Edited by Edward Grube. Scripture quotations: NIV®. Used by permission of Zondervan. All rights reserved. Catechism quotations: *Luther's Small Catechism with Explanation*, © 1986, 1991 CPH. Copyright © 2000 CPH. Printed in U.S.A.

22-2874

Worship the Lord your God, and serve Him only.

Matthew 4:10

Camp Wonderment Rules

1. Hike only on marked camp trails.
2. Always hike or swim with a buddy.
3. Use respectful language toward the counselor and all campers.
4. Show respect in all actions toward counselors, cooks, custodians, and all other camp authorities.
5. Lights out at 10:30 P.M.
6. Help and support other campers however you can.
7. Speak kindly of other campers and encourage each other.
8. Respect the property and belongings of other campers.
9. Attendance at daily camp chapel services is required.
10. IN ALL SITUATIONS, THE RULING OF THE CAMP COUNSELOR IS FINAL.

Camp counselor ABBY, clipboard in hand, stands next to a large tree on the grounds of Camp Wonderment. On the tree is posted a list of rules. ALEX, SEAN, T. J., STEPHANIE, and KARA stand in a semicircle in front of the tree looking at the list and talking among themselves. SEAN plays with his yo-yo as he listens to the others. JESS stands behind the rest of the group with a large scowl on her face. The campers' duffle bags, backpacks, and sleeping bags are in a pile to the right of the group.

Who's in Charge?

KARA: *(Leaning on her crutch)* I wonder what important information Abby has to tell us.

T. J.: Hope it's the times we can swim. I can't wait to dive into that lake!

STEPHANIE: *(Looking toward cabins in the distance)* I hope Abby will say we can move into our cabins. I've got lots of stuff to organize.

ABBY: Attention, everyone! Before we move into our cabins, I'd like to share with you 10 rules we have at Camp Wonderment.

JESS: *(Loudly)* Hrumph!

ABBY looks at JESS. The other campers turn and look at her too.

ABBY: Jess, is something wrong?

JESS: *(Sarcastically sweet)* Oh no, Abby. What could be wrong? *(Mutters)* Only 10 rules that take all the fun out of camping.

ALEX: *(Turns back toward ABBY)* Never mind her, Abby. She always does this at school. If you ignore her, maybe she'll go away.

ABBY: *(Sighs)* Well, campers, I can see we've got a lot of work to do. Jess, these rules aren't meant to ruin your fun. They were written to keep you safe. And some of the rules, Alex, were written to help you treat each other and the counselors with respect.

ALEX: *(Looks down at his feet)* I'm sorry, Abby. Sorry too, Jess.

JESS glares at ALEX. ABBY looks at JESS for a moment.

ABBY: *(Pointing to the list of rules)* As you can see, Rules 1 and 2 tell you to hike only on the trails and to always hike and swim with a friend.

KARA: So we don't get into poison ivy or get lost, right?

ABBY: Exactly. Rules 3 and 4 show how to respect others. Rules 6, 7, and 8 further explain that respect in terms of showing kindness and encouragement and of respecting others' property. I promise to respect you in what I say and do because I care about you and …

JESS: *(Interrupts angrily)* If you respect us so much, then what about Rule 10? If whatever you decide is always the final word, then you don't respect *our* views!

ABBY: *(Patiently)* That's not what Rule 10 means, Jess. I've camped here since I was 10 years old, and I was trained as a camp counselor. Situations may come up when you'll need the advice of someone like me, someone with experience. Because I care about you, I promise I'll look at all sides of a situation before I ever make any decisions. Trust me. I'll be fair.

T. J.: *(Turns to JESS)* What is it with you anyway?

JESS: *(Strongly)* Just looking out for our rights. I don't appreciate rules being crammed down my throat, especially when I've only been here 20 minutes. I get enough of that at home.

ABBY: *(Turns toward group)* Does anyone else have questions about the camp rules?

SEAN: *(Shyly)* When do we eat? Something sure smells good!

ABBY: *(Chuckles and looks at her watch)* In about half an hour, Sean. Those grilled burgers do smell delicious! We've got just enough time to put our gear in our cabins. Then we'll head to the mess hall for lunch. Let's gather up our stuff. Remember, girls in cabin 7 with me, boys in cabin 5. *(ABBY EXITS.)*

T. J.: C'mon, Alex and Sean! First one to the cabin gets the best bunk!

T. J., SEAN, and ALEX grab their bags and EXIT racing. JESS grabs her backpack and EXITS stomping. KARA and STEPHANIE slowly pick up their gear.

STEPHANIE: *(Turns to KARA)* I think we're in for a rough couple of weeks with that Jess. I can't believe how rude she is to Abby.

KARA: Maybe if we tried to be friendly, she'd lighten up a little.

STEPHANIE: I'm staying as far away from her as possible.

KARA: *(Staring after JESS)* I wonder what's making Jess so angry?

STEPHANIE: *(Shrugs)* Who knows? *(Pauses)* We'd better move. I've got lots to do before lunch. *(Picks up her bags and EXITS)*

KARA: Me too. *(Quietly to herself)* And that includes finding out about Jess. *(Slings her pack over her shoulder and EXITS, hobbling with her crutch after STEPHANIE)*

My Life in Jesus

Think about what Abby told the campers about the Camp Wonderment rules. Why did she say the rules were written? How do actual rules in your own life fulfill these same purposes?

How do people around you react to rules in homes, schools, communities, and nations? Have you ever noticed any reactions like Jess's? Why do people rebel against rules?

What is the formal name for the rules God has given His people? Name, if you can, some of these rules. How do these rules benefit you?

The Second Commandment

You shall not misuse the name of the Lord your God.

What does this mean? We should fear and love God so that we do not curse, swear, use satanic arts, lie, or deceive by His name, but call upon it in every trouble, pray, praise, and give thanks.

What is God's name?

God, as He has revealed Himself to us, His essence (who He is) and His attributes (what He is like).

How is God's name misused?

God's name is misused when people speak God's name uselessly or carelessly, curse, swear, use satanic arts, lie, or deceive by His name.

What does God require of us in the Second Commandment?

We should call upon His name in every trouble, pray, praise, and give thanks.

Life Point

We call God our good Father with love and respect because He cares for us and gives us all good things in Jesus.

MY LIFE IN JESUS STUDENT LEAFLETS are published by Concordia Publishing House, 3558 S. Jefferson Ave., St. Louis, MO 63118-3968. Skit scripts written by Diane Grebing. Edited by Edward Grube. Scripture quotations: NIV®. Used by permission of Zondervan. All rights reserved. Catechism quotations: *Luther's Small Catechism with Explanation,* © 1986, 1991 CPH. Copyright © 2000 CPH. Printed in U.S.A.

22-2874

Praise the LORD, O my soul; all my inmost being, praise His holy name.
Psalm 103:1

JESS, STEPHANIE, and KARA enter their cabin. They carry their camp gear. They look around at the three remaining bunk beds as they decide where each will sleep.

Sticks and Stones

STEPHANIE: Okay, roomies! Since Kara's got a hurt knee, it looks like she needs a bottom bunk.

KARA: Thanks, Stephanie, for thinking about me. (*Picks up her sleeping bag, hobbles to the bottom bunk, and sits down*)

JESS: (*To KARA*) Hey, gimp! Why would you ever want to come to a place like this with your knee all torn up?

KARA: It doesn't hold me back too much. I just can't move very fast. The doctor said it would be good for me to be in a place where I can exercise it outside. By the way, my name's Kara, not "gimp."

JESS: Oh, don't take it so personally. How'd you hurt it?

KARA: I tore some ligaments playing softball.

STEPHANIE: So, Jess, which top bunk do you want?

JESS: Anyone but the one over Miss Know-It-All.

STEPHANIE: Who?

JESS: You know, crabby Abby. The farther away from her I can be, the better. I don't know why she thinks she can tell us what to do.

KARA: Because she's the camp counselor, that's why.

JESS: (*Sarcastically*) I suppose if she told you to jump in the lake, you'd do it?

KARA: If she had a good enough reason. (*Pauses, then asks tentatively*) How come you're so against her, Jess? Ever since you've stepped off the bus, you've been so angry.

JESS: (*Defensively*) Just mind your own business, okay? I get really tired of people like you who always want to know what's wrong or what's the matter. Just leave me alone! (*Turns and starts to fix her bunk*)

STEPHANIE: (*Quietly to KARA*) I told you to leave her alone.

KARA, JESS, and STEPHANIE quietly fix their bunks and unpack their gear. ABBY ENTERS the cabin, carrying a large box. She sets it down near her bunk.

ABBY: (*Cheerfully*) I see you're getting settled.

KARA: What's in the box, Abby?

JESS: For such a little gimp, you sure have a big nose!

KARA: I told you, Jess, my name's Kara. I'm sorry you're so unhappy, but you don't have to take it out on me.

ABBY: Girls, let's not forget about the rules. Remember, "speak kindly of other campers and encourage each other."

JESS: Look, Miss Know-It-All, what makes you the big rule master? I don't have to listen to you or to anybody. (*EXITS quickly*)

ABBY stands still for a moment with her head bowed. STEPHANIE and KARA look embarrassed. After a short time, STEPHANIE speaks up.

STEPHANIE: I can't believe Jess! She's got a lot of nerve, talking to you like that and calling you those names.

ABBY: (*Gently*) I don't think it's nerve that makes Jess do that. (*Pauses*) Girls, we've got a problem here. Would you both pray with me? I need God's help to know what to do.

ABBY, STEPHANIE, and KARA fold their hands and bow their heads.

ABBY: Heavenly Father, You know what's in our hearts and minds. I don't know how to help Jess. Her names and words hurt me and make me upset. I know yelling and punishment aren't the answer. Please give me the patience and wisdom I need so I'll know how to help her. In Jesus' name, Amen. (*Pauses and looks at her watch*) Girls, you'd better head over to the mess hall for lunch. After lunch we'll meet at the chapel by the lake. I need to go round up T. J., Alex, and Sean and look for Jess. Thanks for praying with me.

ABBY EXITS.

KARA: I hope Abby will find a way to work things out with Jess.

STEPHANIE: The Bible says all things are possible with God. It's sure gonna take His power to fix this mess!

KARA and STEPHANIE EXIT.

My *Life* in Jesus

Whoever coined the phrase "Sticks and stones may break my bones, but words will never hurt me" must never have experienced what Kara and Abby did. Why is it so important that we seek God's help to control the words we speak?

How can name-calling undermine authority?

Think about the words you've said to others today. Were they encouraging or discouraging? How can God help you with words you use?

The Third Commandment

Remember the Sabbath day by keeping it holy.

What does this mean? We should fear and love God so that we do not despise preaching and His Word, but hold it sacred and gladly hear and learn it.

What is the Sabbath day?

In the Old Testament God set aside the seventh day (Saturday) as a required day of rest (*Sabbath* means "rest") and worship.

Does God require us to observe the Sabbath and other holy days of the Old Testament?

The Sabbath was a sign pointing to Jesus, who is our rest. Since Jesus has come as our Savior and Lord, God no longer requires us to observe the Sabbath day and other holy days of the Old Testament.

Does God require the church to worship together on any specific days?

God requires Christians to worship together. He has not specified any particular day. The church worships together especially on Sunday because Christ rose from the dead on Sunday.

What does God require of us in the Third Commandment?

We should hold preaching and the Word of God sacred. We should gladly hear it, learn it, and meditate on it. We should honor and support the preaching and teaching of the Word of God. We should diligently spread the Word of God.

Life Point

At worship, we listen to God speak in His Word and treasure His promise to love and forgive us for Jesus' sake.

MY LIFE IN JESUS STUDENT LEAFLETS are published by Concordia Publishing House, 3558 S. Jefferson Ave., St. Louis, MO 63118-3968. Skit scripts written by Diane Grebing. Edited by Edward Grube. Scripture quotations: NIV®. Used by permission of Zondervan. All rights reserved. Catechism quotations: *Luther's Small Catechism with Explanation,* © 1986, 1991 CPH. Copyright © 2000 CPH. Printed in U.S.A.

22-2874

Let the word of Christ dwell in you richly as you teach and admonish one another … and as you sing psalms, hymns and spiritual songs with gratitude in your hearts to God. *Colossians 3:16*

ABBY, T. J., SEAN, ALEX, STEPHANIE, KARA, and *JESS sit together at the Camp Wonderment chapel. Everyone but JESS seems joyful. JESS sits at the end of the row, a short distance away from KARA. JESS has a confused look on her face. The CAMP CHAPLAIN stands behind the altar.*

A Chapel Challenge

CHAPLAIN: *(Hands upraised in blessing)* Blessings, campers, on your day! May God be with you! *(EXITS)*

ABBY, ALEX, SEAN, T. J., STEPHANIE, KARA (with her crutch), and JESS leave the chapel. ABBY sings Colossians 3:16 to the tune of "Frère Jacques." THE CAMPERS echo each of the first three lines and sing the last line with ABBY, except JESS, who walks along quietly.

Let Christ's words (Let Christ's words)
Dwell in you. (Dwell in you.)
Teaching with all wisdom (Teaching with all wisdom)
We will praise You, dear God.

ALEX: I really liked those words the chaplain read from Acts about how the disciples met every day to study God's Word, and praise Him. Kind of like what we just did.

ABBY: I like those words too. The Christians in the early church gained a lot of strength and comfort when they gathered together like that.

KARA: I liked the songs. They were so joyful and so much fun to sing!

T. J.: That's aways my favorite part of church. I'm in the youth choir at my church. Our director sometimes gives us rhythm instruments to accent the music when we sing. It sounds pretty cool.

SEAN: *(Quietly)* I liked the prayer. Everything is really new to me here. I was kind of worried about coming to camp. It made me feel better to pray to God with everyone else.

ABBY: *(Putting her arm around SEAN)* God always hears our prayers. It's pretty special to pray with so many others all at once. That always makes me feel closer to other believers.

STEPHANIE: Who made those banners hanging over the altar?

ABBY: Every year the campers make two banners to use during the next camp season. Last year's campers designed those banners.

STEPHANIE: *(Excitedly)* I really like them! My Sunday school class made a banner for my church at home. We used white and gold cloth to make angels that surrounded the words "He is risen!" The pastor hung it by the altar on Easter Sunday.

ABBY: Banners are a great way to express our joy to God for sending Jesus as our Savior. *(Pauses to wipe her brow)* Boy, it's warm today! Let's sit down for a moment by this tree. *(Sits cross-legged on the ground. The other campers sit.)* Did you know Easter's why we worship— especially on Sunday?

T. J.: That's because Jesus rose from the dead on a Sunday. Mom always says every Sunday is like a "little Easter."

JESS: *(Looking down while stirring her finger in the dirt)* I didn't understand much of what was going on at chapel. All that singing and praying—why can't we just do that by ourselves?

ABBY: You can always sing and pray to God on your own, Jess. But worship is a time God designed so we can praise Him with other Christians. At worship we have the benefit of a pastor or chaplain to lead us, to read God's Word, and to explain the Word for our lives.

KARA: We also get to pray for each other at worship. When I hurt my knee, I really appreciated everyone's prayers for healing.

T. J.: It's a lot more fun singing with others than it is by yourself.

STEPHANIE: I like worship at church because it's a time when my mom and dad and my sisters and I get to be together.

SEAN: The best thing about worship is that we focus on what Jesus did and continues to do for us. When I see the cross, sing the hymns, and listen to the Bible readings, I remember that Jesus died for *me* and He came alive again for *me* so that I can have eternal life, forgiveness, and all of God's blessings.

ABBY: Well said, Sean!

JESS: Fine for you, but why do we need to attend chapel every day?

ALEX: It figures you'd say that, Jess. Since you're not in school half the time, I'm sure you'll ditch chapel too.

JESS: *(Glaring at ALEX)* Just shut up, Alex! You don't understand.

ABBY: *(Sternly)* Alex, we're here at camp. School attendance doesn't matter. *(Looking directly at JESS)* I know the chaplain has lots of fun things planned for our chapel times. You might be surprised, Jess, at how much you'll enjoy it.

JESS shrugs and looks down. ALL EXIT.

My Life in Jesus

What benefits do you receive from worship?
Why does God commands His people to worship together?
What are some things you do to focus on God and His goodness when you worship?

The Fourth Commandment

Honor your father and your mother.

What does this mean? We should fear and love God so that we do not despise or anger our parents and other authorities, but honor them, serve and obey them, love and cherish them.

Who are parents and other authorities?

Parents are fathers, mothers, and guardians; other authorities are all those whom God has placed over us at home, in government, at school, at the place where we work, and in the church.

What does God forbid in the Fourth Commandment?

God forbids us to despise our parents and other authorities by not respecting them or angering them by our disobedience or by any other kind of sin.

What does God require of us in the Fourth Commandment?

God requires us
- to honor our parents and other authorities by regarding them as God's representatives;
- to serve our parents and other authorities by gladly providing what they need or require;
- to obey our parents and other authorities in everything in which God has placed them over us; and
- to love and cherish our parents and other authorities as precious gifts of God.

Life Point

We treat our parents and authorities as gifts whom God has given to love and care for us.

MY LIFE IN JESUS STUDENT LEAFLETS are published by Concordia Publishing House, 3558 S. Jefferson Ave., St. Louis, MO 63118-3968. Skit scripts written by Diane Grebing. Edited by Edward Grube. Scripture quotations: NIV®. Used by permission of Zondervan. All rights reserved. Catechism quotations: *Luther's Small Catechism with Explanation*, © 1986, 1991 CPH. Copyright © 2000 CPH. Printed in U.S.A.

22-2874

Children, obey your parents in the Lord, for this is right.
Ephesians 6:1

KARA, ALEX, ABBY, T. J., STEPHANIE, SEAN, and JESS are standing in front of the boys' cabin around a cooler of soft drinks. They are chatting together as each drinks a can of soda. As usual, JESS stands slightly away from the others, but is listening intently to their conversation.

A Revealing Talk

ABBY: So, campers, tell me about your families.

STEPHANIE: We live in an apartment. Mom's a teacher, dad works for the post office, and Zach is my little brother.

ALEX: We live with my grandma because my dad died in an accident when I was three years old. Grandma took care of my brother Jake and me when we were younger so my mom could work as a nurse.

T. J.: My dad works at a bank, and my mom works at a bookstore.

KARA: *(Leaning on a crutch)* I've got three younger sisters. Sharon's in fourth grade; Tasha and Teri are twins. They'll start kindergarten this fall. Mom works at home. Dad drives a truck cross-country.

SEAN: My sister Lisa and I live with my grandma and grandpa. My grandparents own a small store in our neighborhood.

KARA: How about you, Abby? Stephanie, Jess, and I noticed a picture by your bunk. Is that your family?

ABBY: Yes, that picture was taken when my older brother, Cory, graduated from college. He's in medical school now. My dad's a doctor, too, and my mom works as a pharmacist. I also have a younger sister, Sydney. She's a junior in high school and works as a lifeguard. *(Looking at JESS)* Jess, why don't you tell us about your family?

JESS: *(Mumbles and looks at ground)* There's not much to tell. It's just my mom, dad, and my younger brother, Cody.

ABBY: *(To the group)* Thanks for sharing, everyone. Now I want to tell you about a Camp Wonderment tradition. We always ask the campers to write a note home. It sure makes moms, dads, and caregivers feel a lot better when they know you're having a good time here. It also gives you a chance to tell them how much you love and appreciate them. *(Hands out paper, pencils, and envelopes)* When you get your note finished, seal it inside the envelope, add your home address, and give it back to me. I'll stamp it and put it in the mailbox.

THE CAMPERS put their soda cans on the cooler and get their supplies.

KARA: Hey, Jess! Come back to the cabin with us to write your note.

JESS: Nah, I'll just write it by myself over on the bench.

KARA: *(Shrugs)* Suit yourself! C'mon, Stephanie, let's go.

KARA, STEPHANIE, T. J., ALEX, and SEAN EXIT. JESS sits down on the bench by herself. She lays the writing supplies beside her on the bench and stares blankly. ABBY places the soda cans inside the cooler, then walks over to JESS.

ABBY: *(Standing beside the bench)* When you've only been gone from home for a short time, it's hard to know what to write, isn't it?

JESS: *(Glancing up at ABBY)* Writing's not really my thing, you know.

ABBY: Just a few sentences will do.

JESS: *(Bluntly)* I don't think my parents would be interested.

ABBY: What makes you say that, Jess?

JESS: My mom and dad don't care about me. They travel a lot for their jobs, so my brother and I are pretty much on our own. They shipped him off to sports camp and sent me here so they wouldn't have to be bothered with us. To me, this letter is a joke. Why should I show any appreciation for them when they don't show any to me or Cody?

ABBY: *(Thoughtfully)* I'm sorry, Jess. Have you ever told them in a respectful way how you feel? Sometimes parents get so wrapped up in their jobs that they forget that kids just want to hang out with them.

JESS: *(Sarcastically)* You wouldn't understand. I'm sure that your parents are always there for you. Your mom's probably got photo albums and scrapbooks all about you. Your dad's probably there to talk whenever you need him. My mom and dad aren't into that "parent thing." So I don't need to write this stupid note.

JESS wads up the writing paper and throws it on the ground. She crosses her arms angrily over her chest. ABBY puts her hand on JESS's shoulder.

ABBY: It's okay if you don't want to write a note home. But please think about something. God loves us even when we sin against Him. Nobody's parents are perfect, just like we aren't perfect. God helps us show His love to others, even when they don't show us much love. Our parents and caregivers, as imperfect as they might be, are gifts to us from Him.

ABBY EXITS. JESS picks up the crumpled paper, smooths it out, and begins to write.

My *Life* in Jesus

How are your parents and caregivers God's gifts?

Why is it sometimes hard to think of parents and caregivers as blessings?

How do Jess's comments in this skit give you insight into her behavior at camp? If you could talk to Jess, what thoughts, based on your faith in Jesus, might you share with her?

The Fifth Commandment

You shall not murder.

What does this mean? We should fear and love God so that we do not hurt or harm our neighbor in his body, but help and support him in every physical need.

What does God forbid in the Fifth Commandment?

- God forbids us to take the life of another person (murder, abortion, euthanasia) or our own life (suicide);
- God forbids us to hurt or harm our neighbor physically, that is, to do or say anything which may destroy, shorten, or make his or her life bitter;
- God forbids us to keep anger and hatred in our hearts against our neighbor.

What does God require of us in the Fifth Commandment?

- We should help and support our neighbor in every bodily need.
- We should be merciful, kind, and forgiving towards our neighbor.
- We should avoid and assist our neighbor in avoiding the abuse of drugs and the use of any substance that harms the body and the mind.

Life Point

Human life is a gift from God that we treasure and preserve in our thoughts, words, and actions.

[God] Himself gives all men life and breath and everything else. *Acts 17:25*

MY LIFE IN JESUS STUDENT LEAFLETS are published by Concordia Publishing House, 3558 S. Jefferson Ave., St. Louis, MO 63118-3968. Skit scripts written by Diane Grebing. Edited by Edward Grube. Scripture quotations: NIV®. Used by permission of Zondervan. All rights reserved. Catechism quotations: *Luther's Small Catechism with Explanation,* © 1986, 1991 CPH. Copyright © 2000 CPH. Printed in U.S.A.

22-2874

The campers are gathered with ABBY in a big clearing on the grounds of Camp Wonderment. They are talking among themselves as they look around the clearing at the different stations of an endurance coarse.

Angry Words

ABBY: (Blows whistle) Okay, campers! Time for some fun! (Gestures behind her) Welcome to the Camp Wonderment Endurance Course. Around the clearing you'll notice 10 stations of athletic equipment. As you proceed through each activity, I'll time how long it takes our group to finish. Later we'll compare our scores with the other groups. The group with the fastest time wins a trophy and an ice-cream party.

STEPHANIE: What kinds of things do we have to do?

ABBY: There's some running, climbing, and jumping events.

KARA: (Waves her crutch with disappointment) I guess that leaves me out.

ABBY: On some of the events, yes. But I'll need someone to record our times and help me cheer the group on.

KARA: (Brightens) I can do that!

ABBY: The first station's over there at the balance beam. C'mon! Let's go!

The group follows ABBY to the balance beam. ALEX lags behind.

T. J.: (Looks back at ALEX) C'mon, man! Hurry up! We're going to get the best time this camp's ever seen.

ALEX: (Crossly) I'll get there when I get there. You go ahead and start.

The group gathers at the balance beam. ALEX brings up the rear.

ABBY: The object is to see how quickly our group can cross the beam. You'll line up at this end. When Kara and I get to the other end, I'll yell "GO!" Then follow each other across the beam. The time will stop when everyone walks across with no falls. Understand?

JESS, T. J., STEPHANIE, SEAN, and ALEX line up at the far end of the beam. KARA and ABBY go to the other end. ABBY pulls out a stopwatch.

ABBY: (Yelling) On your mark, get set, GO!

JESS jumps on the beam and runs across it quickly. T. J. follows easily. STEPHANIE follows more slowly but reaches the end with no falls. KARA and ABBY cheer. JESS and T. J. join them, as does STEPHANIE. SEAN moves slowly across the beam with a look of concentration on his face.

KARA: You're almost there, Sean. Go for it!

SEAN finishes with a smile. ALEX steps up on the beam, arms flailing. After a few steps he falls off, runs back to the start, and tries again.

KARA: That's okay, Alex. You're doin' great!

ALEX falls off the beam again.

T. J.: (To JESS) What a klutz! (Directly to ALEX) C'mon, you loser!

ALEX: (Angrily) You can just drop dead, T. J.! And that goes for the rest of you too. Who cares about this stupid endurance course anyway!

ALEX runs to the far left side of the stage and stands with his back to the group.

ABBY: (Firmly) T. J., we're a team here. Everyone is valuable.

T. J.: Yeah, but he told all of us, even you, to "drop dead." I guess he doesn't think we're too valuable either.

ABBY: Alex shouldn't have said that. "Drop dead" are powerful words. (Hands the stopwatch to KARA) I need to talk to Alex.

CAMPERS stand with their heads bowed. ABBY goes over to ALEX.

ABBY: (Quietly) Alex? I think we need to talk.

ALEX looks up slowly at ABBY as he quickly wipes a tear away.

ALEX: I was trying my best, Abby. Please don't be mad at me for ruining the time. I'm just not very coordinated, I guess.

ABBY: Alex. I'm upset because you told all of us to "drop dead."

ALEX: I just couldn't stand it when T. J. started yelling at me.

ABBY: "Drop dead" are powerful words, Alex. God's given each of us our lives. We're each of great value to Him. God wants us to value each other.

ALEX: I'm sorry, Abby. I guess I didn't think.

ABBY: (Putting her arm around ALEX's shoulder) I forgive you, Alex. Let's get back to the others. I've got some tips to help you tackle that balance beam.

ABBY and ALEX walk back to the group.

T. J.: I'm sorry I made fun of you. It wasn't right.

ALEX: (To the group) I'm sorry I said what I did. I let my anger and pride take over. I wouldn't want anything bad to happen to you.

THE CAMPERS gather at the end of the balance beam for another try.

My Life in Jesus

Violent words and actions are sinful. Why are violent *thoughts* also sinful?

When you are angry, what are some ways to handle such feelings so that you don't sin in your thoughts, words, and actions?

Think of someone in your school who gets picked on by other students. What is a kind and genuine compliment you could offer to build this person up with Christ's love? Plan to share this comment with this person at an appropriate time.

The Sixth Commandment

You shall not commit adultery.

What does this mean? We should fear and love God so that we lead a sexually pure and decent life in what we say and do, and husband and wife love and honor each other.

How do we lead a sexually pure and decent life?

We lead a sexually pure and decent life when we

- consider sexuality to be a good gift of God;
- honor marriage as God's institution, the lifelong union of one man and one woman;
- reserve sexual intercourse for the marriage partner alone;
- control sexual urges in a God-pleasing way.

What does God require of us in the Sixth Commandment?

- God requires us to avoid all temptations to sexual sin.
- God requires us to be clean in what we think and say.
- God requires us to use our sexuality in ways pleasing to Him.

Do you not know that your body is a temple of the Holy Spirit? ... Therefore honor God with your body. *1 Corinthians 6:19–20*

Life Point

Our sexuality is a good gift of God to be enjoyed and controlled in God-pleasing ways throughout our lives and in marriage.

ALEX and T. J. stand by a bulletin board inside the camp recreation building. They are looking at some photographs posted on the board. ALEX and T. J. point at several of the pictures and laugh. SEAN and KARA stands slightly away from them, watching them with an embarrassed expression.

JESS and STEPHANIE, ENTER, talking with each other.

MY LIFE IN JESUS STUDENT LEAFLETS are published by Concordia Publishing House, 3558 S. Jefferson Ave., St. Louis, MO 63118-3968. Skit scripts written by Diane Grebing. Edited by Edward Grube. Scripture quotations: NIV®. Used by permission of Zondervan. All rights reserved. Catechism quotations: *Luther's Small Catechism with Explanation,* © 1986, 1991 CPH. Copyright © 2000 CPH. Printed in U.S.A.

22-2874

Physique 101

STEPHANIE: *(Giggles)* Did either of you see that blond guy from cabin 2? What a babe! *(KARA and JESS nod in agreement)*

JESS: *(Gesturing toward the boys)* I wonder what Alex, T. J., and Sean are looking at over there.

The girls walk over to the boys at the bulletin board.

ALEX: *(Looks over his shoulder)* Shhh! The girls are coming.

KARA: Hi, guys. What are you looking at?

T. J.: Nothing! *(Bursts out laughing, joined by ALEX)*

JESS: The way you two are laughing, it must be something. Let us see. *(Elbows her way between the boys)* It's a bunch of pictures.

KARA: *(Edges to the bulletin board)* I wonder if these are pictures of people who've camped here before.

STEPHANIE: I remember this from last summer. Every year they add new pictures, but some pictures here are from 15 years ago. *(Looks intently at the board)* I wonder … oh, there it is! *(Points at a picture)* Here's me, Shannon, and Kris from last summer down by the lake.

T. J.: Nice legs, Stephanie! *(Jabs ALEX in the ribs with his elbow)*

STEPHANIE blushes and backs away. ABBY ENTERS unnoticed.

T. J.: *(Points at another picture)* Hey, get a load of this porker! I bet when she jumped in the lake, half the water came out!

ALEX: *(Pointing and laughing)* Look, T. J., there she is again. I'm surprised there was room for anyone else in that picture!

ABBY: Do you know who that girl is that you were pointing out?

The group turns around abruptly, realizing ABBY is there with them.

ABBY: I asked you a question. Do you know who that girl is?

T. J.: *(Looking down at his feet)* No.

ABBY: That's me, the first year I came to camp, eight summers ago.

ALEX: *(Amazedly)* You're kidding! That can't possibly be you!

ABBY: Yes it is. *(Points at another picture)* Here I am the next year *(points at another photo)* and the year after that. In three years I grew five inches taller. *(Pauses)* I'm a little amazed by your comments, guys.

ALEX and T. J. look embarrassed.

JESS: Guys can be such jerks. They're always making fun of girls who aren't skinny and cute.

KARA: If somebody doesn't look like a fashion model, they call her a "dog" or some other stupid name. I just don't get it.

ABBY: Now wait a minute, girls. I seem to recall the three of you going talking about a "babe" in cabin 2?

The girls look embarrassed.

SEAN: *(To ABBY)* How come everybody's always so hung up on how people look? Some of the stuff people say really hurts.

ABBY: God has made us all different. My pictures show that I've been several sizes already. God wants us to take care of our physical bodies, but also our thoughts, actions, and beliefs about our bodies.

STEPHANIE: That's hard when every magazine you look at shows girls in size 2 clothes and boys that look like Olympic athletes.

ABBY: Books, magazines, TV shows, and movies often belittle and ruin the beauty of the bodies God has created. God especially cares about us inside, the beauty of our hearts. In Jesus, He sees us as His pure and holy children.

T. J.: *(Mumbles)* We were only joking around. We're sorry.

ABBY: I forgive you. Respectful use of our bodies is a big deal. But the best blessings God gives are forgiveness and eternal life in Jesus. God's forgiveness makes our *hearts* pure. It all comes down to love, honor, and respect—for God and for other people. *(Checks watch)* Wow, it's almost 10 o'clock. We'd better get back to our cabins.

ABBY, STEPHANIE, SEAN, and KARA EXIT. As T. J. and ALEX stare at the bulletin board, JESS walks over to them.

JESS: I'm starting to understand why they call this place Camp Wonderment. Abby's always talking about God. I thought this was just a summer camp. I wonder what this place really is all about.

ALEX, T. J., and JESS EXIT together.

My Life in Jesus

How do the comments you've heard from kids concerning their bodies and the bodies of others compare to those made by the campers?

Carefully read 1 Corinthians 6:19–20, found on page 1.

How are our bodies "temples"? How can we honor God with our bodies?

How do you think television programs, movies, and magazines present the body and sexuality? How do these worldly views compare to God's desire for His people?

In everything, do to others what you would have them do to you.
Matthew 7:12

The Seventh Commandment

You shall not steal.

What does this mean? We should fear and love God so that we do not take our neighbor's money or possessions, or get them in any dishonest way, but help him to improve and protect his possessions and income.

What does God forbid in the Seventh Commandment?

God forbids every kind of robbery, theft, and dishonest way of getting things.

What does God require of us in the Seventh Commandment?

• We should help our neighbor to improve and protect that person's possessions and income.
• We should help our neighbor in every need.

Life Point

We help others preserve and protect their money and possessions as we recognize that such things are gifts from God.

MY LIFE IN JESUS STUDENT LEAFLETS are published by Concordia Publishing House, 3558 S. Jefferson Ave., St. Louis, MO 63118-3968. Skit scripts written by Diane Grebing. Edited by Edward Grube. Scripture quotations: NIV®. Used by permission of Zondervan. All rights reserved. Catechism quotations: *Luther's Small Catechism with Explanation,* © 1986, 1991 CPH. Copyright © 2000 CPH. Printed in U.S.A.

22-2874

ALEX, SEAN, and T. J. are in their cabin, getting ready for bed. ALEX and T. J. are sitting on their bunk bed. SEAN stands next to the bed doing yo-yo tricks. ALEX and T. J. watch SEAN.

The Yo-Yo Trick (Part 1)

ALEX: Hey, you're pretty good with that thing.

T. J.: He oughta be. Sean practices three or four hours a day.

SEAN: (*Grins and flings the yo-yo up and down*) Nah, not that much.

ALEX: Where did you get that yo-yo?

SEAN: My grandpa bought it for me for my birthday. Want me to show you how to do the gravity gripper?

ALEX: Okay. (*Gets out of his bunk and stands next to SEAN. SEAN slips the yo-yo string on Alex's middle finger.*)

SEAN: Just snap your wrist downward so your palm is out as you throw the yo-yo down. Then snap your wrist back up to catch it.

ALEX tries it. The yo-yo drops to the ground with the string extended.

T. J.: (*Laughing*) Great job, Alex!

SEAN: (*Patiently to ALEX*) It takes a little practice. Give me the yo-yo so I can wind the string for you. Then you can give it another try.

SEAN rewinds the yo-yo and gives it back to ALEX. ALEX tries again, this time bringing the yo-yo back up in his palm successfully.

SEAN: (*Loudly*) That's it! You're getting the hang of it.

ABBY: (*From offstage*) Boys! It's 10:30. Lights out!

SEAN: I guess we'll have to wait until tomorrow. (*Yawns and gets into his bunk*) Just put my yo-yo in my backpack, would you, Alex?

ALEX: Sure. (*Walks to SEAN's backpack but sticks the yo-yo in his pocket*)

ALEX and T. J. get in their bunks.

Snoring is heard. A STUDENT walks across the stage spinning the hands of a clock to indicate time passing. Offstage an alarm clock rings. ALEX, T. J., and SEAN get out of bed and pantomime getting dressed.

ABBY: (*Calling from outside the cabin*) Sean! Alex! T. J.! Time for breakfast!

T. J. and ALEX head toward the cabin door. SEAN rifles through his backpack.

T. J.: (*Looking back at SEAN*) C'mon, Sean. Let's go eat.

SEAN: Alex, where did you put my yo-yo? It's not in my backpack.

ALEX: (*Fingering the pocket where he has the yo-yo and speaking quietly*) I'm sure it's in there. You just don't see it.

T. J.: (*Impatiently*) Aw, look for it later. My stomach's growling.

SEAN: (*Shrugs*) I guess you're right. It must be in here somewhere. It couldn't have gotten up and walked off on its own.

SEAN follows ALEX and T. J. out of the cabin, where they meet ABBY. As they walk, ALEX lags behind and fingers his pocket. Suddenly ALEX stops.

ALEX: You guys go on ahead. I forgot to uh, uh, uh, comb my hair. I'll catch up with you in a minute. (*Turns and runs back to the cabin*)

T. J., SEAN, and ABBY wait impatiently.

ABBY: T. J., would you please go back and see what's keeping Alex?

T. J.: Sure, Abby. (*Runs back to cabin and enters. ALEX turns around quickly with a guilty look.*) What's taking you so … (*Sees the yo-yo in ALEX's hand*) Hey, that's Sean's. What are you doing with it?

ALEX: Uh, uh, nothing. Just trying it out.

T. J.: (*Stares at ALEX*) Did you take that out of Sean's backpack?

ALEX: No, I never put it back last night. I figured Sean wouldn't miss it.

T. J.: That's stealing, Alex.

ALEX: It's just a little yo-yo. Sean will forget all about it.

T. J.: His grandpa gave it to him. You better put it back.

SEAN enters the cabin with ABBY right behind him.

SEAN: (*Sees his yo-yo in ALEX's hand*) Alex! You found my yo-yo! (*Takes the yo-yo*) Thanks! You're a great friend! Where was it, anyway?

ALEX: Uh, under your bed. It must have rolled out of your backpack.

T. J.: (*Muttering*) Some friend you are!

ABBY: What did you say, T. J.?

ALEX: (*Glances at T. J.*) Nothing, Abby. T. J. was just talking about yo-yo tricks.

ABBY: (*Looking at ALEX and T. J. quizzically*) Well, at least the missing yo-yo's been found. C'mon, boys. I hear pancakes calling.

ABBY and SEAN EXIT.

T. J.: I can't believe how you got out of that, Alex.

ALEX: Pretty tricky, huh? *ALEX EXITS.*

T. J.: (*Shaking his head*) If I were Sean, I'd hide that yo-yo! (*EXITS*)

My *Life* in Jesus

In what ways does stealing hurt or harm people?

What leads people to steal others' possessions?

Read carefully the words of **Matthew 7:12** found on page 1. How might these words be used when dealing with a thief?

The meaning of the Seventh Commandment tells us to help protect the possessions of others. Did T. J. fulfill this duty? How might he have handled this situation differently?

The Eighth Commandment

You shall not give false testimony against your neighbor.

What does this mean? We should fear and love God so that we do not tell lies about our neighbor, betray him, slander him, or hurt his reputation, but defend him, speak well of him, and explain everything in the kindest way.

What does God forbid in the Eighth Commandment?

- God forbids us to tell lies about our neighbor in a court of law or elsewhere, that is, to lie about, lie to, or withhold the truth from our neighbor.
- God forbids us to betray our neighbor, that is, to reveal our neighbor's secrets.
- God forbids us to slander our neighbor or hurt our neighbor's reputation.

What does God require of us in the Eighth Commandment?

- We should defend our neighbor, that is, we should speak up for and protect our neighbor from false accusations.
- We should speak well of our neighbor, that is, we should praise our neighbor's good actions and qualities.
- We should put the best meaning on everything, that is, we should explain our neighbor's actions in the best possible way.

Life Point

When we defend and speak well of others at all times, we show them the kind and compassionate love God shows us in Jesus, our Savior.

MY LIFE IN JESUS STUDENT LEAFLETS are published by Concordia Publishing House, 3558 S. Jefferson Ave., St. Louis, MO 63118-3968. Skit scripts written by Diane Grebing. Edited by Edward Grube. Scripture quotations: NIV®. Used by permission of Zondervan. All rights reserved. Catechism quotations: *Luther's Small Catechism with Explanation*, © 1986, 1991 CPH. Copyright © 2000 CPH. Printed in U.S.A.

22-2874

[Love] always protects, always trusts, always hopes, always perseveres.
1 Corinthians 13:7

KARA, STEPHANIE, SEAN, T. J., and ALEX are sitting in the camp mess hall eating breakfast. JESS and ABBY are still getting their food in the cafeteria line. Their backs are turned toward the other campers.

The Trouble with Rumors

STEPHANIE: I've got some hot news about Jess.

ALEX: What hot news?

STEPHANIE: (*Moves in closer and lowers voice*) Last night Jess was on the phone arguing with her mother. She was talking so loud I couldn't help but overhear when she said to her mom, "I'd rather go to Lockwood than be stuck here!"

ALEX: (*Surprised*) She really said she'd rather go to Lockwood?

SEAN: (*Innocently*) What's the big deal about going to Lockwood?

ALEX: It's just the biggest juvenile home in the state! It's in the town of Lockwood about 45 miles away. I've heard some of the kids sent there are killers! I wonder what Jess did to get sent there?

KARA: Are you sure that's what Jess said, Stephanie? Sometimes people are hard to understand when they're angry.

STEPHANIE: Sure I'm sure, Kara. Besides, think about how Jess acts all the time. She's always so mean. It sure wouldn't surprise me … (*Looks up*) Uh-oh, here she comes.

JESS comes up to the camper's table with her food tray. The other campers look down and concentrate on eating their food.

JESS: Good morning! Mind if I sit with you guys?

T. J.: (*Shrugs*) It's a free country.

JESS sits down at the table next to SEAN, who immediately shies away from her. The others move slightly away from JESS as well.

JESS: You guys don't have to move. I showered this morning! (*Pauses*) What's the matter with all of you? You're usually chattering.

ABBY arrives at the table with a full tray. ABBY sits down next to JESS.

ABBY: My, you guys are quiet. Must be this good food!

The campers nod quietly while nervously glancing at Jess.

JESS: Why do you guys keep looking at me? Have I got food on my face?

ABBY: Okay, who wants to tell me what's going on here?

KARA: (*Quietly*) It's okay, Abby. We know all about Jess.

JESS: What do you mean you know all about me?

ALEX: She means we know all about Lockwood.

JESS: Lockwood? How do you know about Lockwood? (*Thinks for a moment, then glares at STEPHANIE*) Were you listening in on my phone conversation last night?

STEPHANIE: (*Looking down*) I couldn't help but hear you.

JESS: (*Slightly embarrassed*) Yeah, mom and I had a fight. But don't tell me you haven't ever had a fight with your parents.

ALEX: Not about going to Lockwood, we haven't.

JESS: What's wrong with Lockwood? My grandparents live there. I always enjoy visiting them. (*Suddenly understands*) Oh, I get it. You guys think I was talking about the juvenile home in Lockwood.

JESS looks appalled, then EXITS with a hurt expression.

ABBY: I can't believe this! Stephanie, come with me.

ABBY gets up from the table and leaves the mess hall. STEPHANIE follows.

ABBY: Jess, please wait up. Stephanie has something to tell you.

JESS stops and turns around.

STEPHANIE: I'm sorry, Jess. I just assumed you meant the juvenile center. (*defensively*) But can you blame me? Look at how you act.

JESS: Well, maybe I haven't exactly acted in a way that would make you think I had a good reputation.

STEPHANIE: I shouldn't have spoken until I had all the facts.

ABBY: You shouldn't have shared anything with anyone even if you did know all the facts, Stephanie. Comments like the ones you made give others the wrong impression about someone's reputation.

STEPHANIE hangs her head. JESS looks at ABBY with surprise.

JESS: How come you're defending me?

ABBY: All of us have things in our lives, Jess, that people can start rumors about. God helps me try to see everyone in a positive way. We all have our faults and we all have our good points too. I try to look for the good.

STEPHANIE: (*To herself*) I really messed up. (*Looks at JESS*) I wonder if Jess can forgive me.

My *Life* in Jesus

What are some of the consequences of rumors?

What responsibilities do we have whenever we speak?

Read carefully 1 Corinthians 13:7 from page 1. How can remembering Christ's love for us help us wisely choose what we say about others?

The Ninth Commandment

You shall not covet your neighbor's house.

What does this mean? We should fear and love God so that we do not scheme to get our neighbor's inheritance or house, or get it in a way which only appears right, but help and be of service to him in keeping it.

The Tenth Commandment

You shall not covet your neighbor's wife, or his manservant or maidservant, his ox or donkey, or anything that belongs to your neighbor.

What does this mean? We should fear and love God so that we do not entice or force away our neighbor's wife, workers, or animals, or turn them against him, but urge them to stay and do their duty.

What is coveting?

Coveting is having a sinful desire for anyone or anything that belongs to our neighbor.

What coveting does God forbid in these commandments?

In the Ninth Commandment, God forbids every sinful desire to get our neighbor's possessions openly or by trickery. In the Tenth Commandment, God forbids every sinful desire to take from our neighbor that person's spouse or workers.

What does God require of us in these commandments?

We should be content with what God has given us and assist our neighbor in keeping what God has given that person. We should be content with the helpers God has given us and encourage our neighbor's helpers to be faithful to our neighbor.

Life Point

We can be satisfied with our earthly possessions and appreciative of the wealth and possessions of others, for God lovingly gives us all good things.

MY LIFE IN JESUS STUDENT LEAFLETS are published by Concordia Publishing House, 3558 S. Jefferson Ave., St. Louis, MO 63118-3968. Skit scripts written by Diane Grebing. Edited by Edward Grube. Scripture quotations: NIV®. Used by permission of Zondervan. All rights reserved. Catechism quotations: *Luther's Small Catechism with Explanation*, © 1986, 1991 CPH. Copyright © 2000 CPH. Printed in U.S.A.   22-2874

Delight yourself in the LORD and He will give you the desires of your heart.   *Psalm 37:4*

SEAN stands outside the cabin area performing yo-yo tricks for T. J., ALEX, STEPHANIE, KARA, JESS, and ABBY, who sit around him. Everyone smiles at SEAN's accomplishments but ALEX, who has a scowl on his face.

The Yo-Yo Trick (Part 2)

ABBY: *(Applauding)* Wow, Sean! T. J. said you were great with that yo-yo!

SEAN performs another trick. All in the group clap but ALEX.

ALEX: Aw, what's the big deal anyway. It's just a stupid yo-yo.

T. J.: *(Taunting)* I thought you liked Sean's "stupid yo-yo," Alex.

ALEX: *(Menacingly)* Get off my case, T. J. If you say anything, I'll …

SEAN: *(Helpfully)* Hey, Alex! Why don't you show everybody the gravity gripper. You had it down pretty well the other night.

ALEX: *(Hesitates)* Well, okay, I guess.

SEAN gives ALEX the yo-yo. ALEX tries the trick, but fails.

JESS: Good job, Alex!

SEAN: *(To JESS)* Give him a break, Jess. These tricks aren't easy. *(Turns to ALEX)* Wind up the string and try again.

ALEX winds up the string and tries again. This time he succeeds.

SEAN: Way to go, Alex. I knew you'd remember.

T. J.: That's enough of this amateur stuff, Alex. Let Sean show us some real tricks.

ALEX: Can't I use it just a little longer, Sean? *(Longingly)* This is the neatest yo-yo I've ever seen. I sure wish I had one like it.

T. J.: Uh-oh.

ABBY: "Uh-oh" what, T. J.?

T. J.: Nothing.

SEAN: It's not a very expensive yo-yo, Alex. Maybe when you get home you can get one for yourself. *(Holds out his hand to ALEX)* C'mon, man, I gave you a turn. Please let me have my yo-yo back.

ALEX: Hey, Sean! I've got an idea. If I can do the gravity gripper perfectly 20 times in a row, will you let me have the yo-yo for keeps?

SEAN: No way! My grandpa gave me that yo-yo for my birthday.

ALEX: How about 30 times? 40? 50?

T. J.: Uh-oh.

STEPHANIE: *(Annoyed)* T. J., why do you keep saying "Uh-oh"?

ALEX: I know I could do it 50 times. What do you say, Sean?

ABBY: Alex, what is going on with you and that yo-yo? Every time you get around it, you start acting really strange.

T. J.: You don't know the half of it.

ABBY: *(Turns to T. J.)* T. J., if you've got something to say, say it.

ALEX shoots T. J. a panicked look and clears his throat loudly.

T. J.: It's nothing, Abby.

ALEX: *(Pleading)* C'mon, Sean. I could do that trick 50 times in a row. I bet that would be a world record. Then I'd deserve the yo-yo.

ABBY: *(Laughs)* Alex, enough is enough. Give Sean his yo-yo.

SEAN: *(Walks up to ALEX)* Give it back. It's mine.

ALEX: *(Clutching the yo-yo above SEAN's head)* Jump for it, Sean.

SEAN jumps up and tries to grab the yo-yo. ABBY walks around behind ALEX and grabs the yo-yo from him.

ABBY: *(Handing the yo-yo back to SEAN)* Here, Sean.

ALEX: Just having a little fun, Abby.

T. J.: Like the other morning, Alex?

ABBY: *(Turns to T. J.)* T. J., 'fess up. What's really going on here?

ALEX frantically shakes his head no.

T. J.: The other morning when Alex went back to the cabin to comb his hair, he really went back to steal Sean's yo-yo.

ABBY: I thought Alex had just found the yo-yo.

T. J.: That's what Alex would like you to think.

ABBY: Alex, it's okay to admire something someone else has, but to plot to take it and then actually steal it …

ALEX: *(With shame)* I know, I know. *(To SEAN)* I'm sorry I took the yo-yo, especially since it was a present from your grandpa.

SEAN: I forgive you, Alex, but I don't think I'll be teaching you any more tricks with it.

SEAN, KARA, STEPHANIE, JESS, and T. J. EXIT to go on a hike.

ALEX: *(With disgust)* Well, Sean doesn't trust me with his yo-yo anymore. I don't think he trusts me as a friend, either.

ABBY: Trust takes a long time to build, but a short time to destroy. Sean's fair-minded. He has Jesus' love in his heart. Jesus' love is forgiving and merciful. Sean said he forgives you. I think maybe in time he'll give you another chance.

ALEX and ABBY EXIT.

My *Life* in Jesus

How did Alex's desire for Sean's yo-yo become coveting?
How does God's love and forgiveness help us show love and forgiveness to others who sin against us?
What are some ways we can keep our desires God-pleasing?

The First Article—*Who Is God?*

The Apostles' Creed

I believe in God, the Father Almighty, Maker of heaven and earth.

And in Jesus Christ, His only Son, our Lord, who was conceived by the Holy Spirit, born of the Virgin Mary, suffered under Pontius Pilate, was crucified, died and was buried. He descended into hell. The third day He rose again from the dead. He ascended into heaven and sits at the right hand of God, the Father Almighty. From thence He will come to judge the living and the dead.

I believe in the Holy Spirit, the holy Christian church, the communion of saints, the forgiveness of sins, the resurrection of the body, and the life everlasting. Amen.

The First Article

I believe in God, the Father Almighty, Maker of heaven and earth.

What does this mean? I believe that God has made me and all creatures; that He has given me my body and soul, eyes, ears, and all my members, my reason and all my senses, and still takes care of them.

He also gives me clothing and shoes, food and drink, house and home, wife and children, land, animals, and all I have. He richly and daily provides me with all that I need to support this body and life.

He defends me against all danger and guards and protects me from all evil.

All this He does only out of fatherly, divine goodness and mercy, without any merit or worthiness in me. For all this it is my duty to thank and praise, serve and obey Him.

This is most certainly true.

Life Point

Christians believe God has made each individual and the entire universe and gives us all that we need.

MY LIFE IN JESUS STUDENT LEAFLETS are published by Concordia Publishing House, 3558 S. Jefferson Ave., St. Louis, MO 63118-3968. Skit scripts written by Diane Grebing. Edited by Edward Grube. Scripture quotations: NIV®. Used by permission of Zondervan. All rights reserved. Catechism quotations: *Luther's Small Catechism with Explanation,* © 1986, 1991 CPH. Copyright © 2000 CPH. Printed in U.S.A.

22-2874

By Him all things were created: things in heaven and on earth, visible and invisible. *Colossians 1:16*

ABBY hikes on a wooded path at Camp Wonderment. She leads ALEX, SEAN, STEPHANIE, JESS, T. J., and KARA.

A Wonder-Filled Walk

ABBY: It's a great day, isn't it, campers?

JESS: *(Swats a mosquito on her leg)* I wish we didn't have all these bugs!

ABBY: They're a part of God's creation, Jess. They feed the birds.

JESS: Then why don't the birds get busy and eat them?

The group follows ABBY, scanning the woods as they hike.

T. J.: *(Stops and points)* Wow, look at that tree! It's huge!

The others gather around T. J. and look in the direction he points.

ABBY: You've discovered "Grandpappy Oak." The owners of the camp think that tree is nearly 100 years old. Does anyone know how you can tell the actual age of a tree?

SEAN: When the tree dies, you can cut open its trunk and count the rings you see on the wood inside. Each ring represents a year.

STEPHANIE: We learned at school that the rings can tell you a lot about a tree's history. Wide rings show that a tree had access to more sunlight and moisture during that year.

ABBY: Sean and Stephanie, you're tree experts! Tree rings are just one of millions of neat little facts about God's creation.

The group hikes on a little farther. ALEX sees an interesting plant a short way off the trail. He leaves the trail to go take a look at it.

ALEX: *(Stands by the plant)* I just noticed this neat plant. See how its leaves are grouped together in threes? *(Reaches down to touch it)*

KARA: Don't touch that, Alex! I think that might be poison ivy. My mom always says, "Leaflets three, let them be."

ABBY: *(Stands next to ALEX)* That's good advice, Kara. You don't want to get poison ivy, Alex. The itching can be pretty miserable. Let's get back on the trail.

The group hikes to the clearing, where they stop to rest.

SEAN: Abby, as I look around at all the trees and plants here, I can't understand how some people don't believe that God made all this.

JESS: Why do all of you keep saying that God made all this? Plants and animals reproduce on their own. They adapt and evolve over millions of years. At least that's what I learned in science at school.

ABBY: Evolution is a theory people use to attempt to explain how the world came to be. To those people, that theory makes more sense than believing the truth that God made and preserves all life and creation.

T. J.: Doesn't that evolution stuff say that a big explosion started the world? I've never understood how blowing something up could make all these wonderful things.

ABBY: Ideas like evolution reject a belief in God as the almighty Creator. As Christians, what we believe is not just something we learn and remember in our minds. It's also something that we believe and accept in *our hearts*. We base our beliefs on the Bible, God's true Word. The Bible says, "By faith we understand that the universe was formed at God's command." Those words from Hebrews 11:3 tell us that it's through faith that we know that God created the world.

SEAN: My grandpa always says that there's no way creation could have happened by chance. He says that when you look at how similar living things are, yet how they also are unique, and when you consider how things work together in nature, it's obvious that someone with vast intelligence, wisdom, and power designed it all.

ABBY: It's just like all the plants we've noticed today and even the mosquitos, Jess. Everything that God has created has a place, a purpose, and a design. Colossians 1:16 tells us, "By Him all things were created: things in heaven and on earth, visible and invisible." What a mighty and awesome God we have!

JESS: *(Gesturing around her)* It seems pretty incredible to me that somebody could just make all this.

ABBY: It is incredible, Jess. Human reasoning can't explain how God made the universe out of nothing and how He did it all in just six days. But through faith, we believe that with God nothing is impossible. From the facts recorded in the Bible, we know it's true.

STEPHANIE: Abby, I think I saw something moving up ahead.

ABBY and THE CAMPERS stand up and continue down the trail.

My *Life* in Jesus

Why do you think it is so hard for some people to believe that God alone created the world?

What are some specific things we can do, by the power of the Holy Spirit, to witness the truths about God's creation?

Think of a specific living thing or geographic feature in God's creation that you think is particularly wonderful. Thank God in prayer for this creation.

The First Article

I believe in God, the Father Almighty, Maker of heaven and earth.

What does this mean? I believe that God has made me and all creatures; that He has given me my body and soul, eyes, ears, and all my members, my reason and all my senses, and still takes care of them.

He also gives me clothing and shoes, food and drink, house and home, wife and children, land, animals, and all I have. He richly and daily provides me with all that I need to support this body and life.

He defends me against all danger and guards and protects me from evil.

All this He does only out of fatherly, divine goodness and mercy, without any merit or worthiness in me. For all this it is my duty to thank and praise, serve and obey Him.

This is most certainly true.

How does the universe still depend on God?

God sustains all things by His wisdom and power.

What does God do to take care of me?

- He gives me food and clothing, home and family, work and play, and all that I need from day to day.
- "He defends me against all danger and guards and protects me from all evil."

Why does God do this for us?

"All this He does out of fatherly, divine goodness and mercy, without any merit or worthiness in me."

Life Point

As Christians, we believe God defends and protects us from danger and evil throughout our lives because we are His beloved children in Jesus.

MY LIFE IN JESUS STUDENT LEAFLETS are published by Concordia Publishing House, 3558 S. Jefferson Ave., St. Louis, MO 63118-3968. Skit scripts written by Diane Grebing. Edited by Edward Grube. Scripture quotations: NIV®. Used by permission of Zondervan. All rights reserved. Catechism quotations: *Luther's Small Catechism with Explanation*, © 1986, 1991 CPH. Copyright © 2000 CPH. Printed in U.S.A.

22-2874

Cast all your anxiety on Him because He cares for you.
1 Peter 5:7

ABBY and THE CAMPERS continue to hike along the nature trail. STEPHANIE has temporarily taken the lead as she charges ahead to investigate something she saw move across the path.

A Rattling Experience

ABBY: Stephanie! Stay with the group please! Occasionally there are some unexpected dangers along this trail.

STEPHANIE: (Calling back to the others) I'm fine, Abby. I think I saw something interesting up ahead. I just want to check it out.

STEPHANIE puts more distance between herself and the others. Suddenly she stops dead in her tracks and lets out a small squeal.

T. J.: I wonder why Stephanie stopped so quickly?

STEPHANIE: (Weakly) Abby? Abby? I think I'm in trouble.

ABBY: (Jogging toward STEPHANIE) What's wrong, Stephanie?

STEPHANIE: (Panicked) Don't, don't, don't come any closer. It's a, a …

ALEX: It's a "a … A"?

KARA: Be quiet, Alex, I think something's really wrong.

ABBY: (Approaches STEPHANIE from behind) Just try to stay calm, Stephanie. (Suddenly notices the creature on the path in front of STEPHANIE) Oh, my, it's a rattlesnake! (Gesturing to the other campers to stop) Everyone, stop! Don't anyone move. Any sudden movements could make the rattlesnake strike out at Stephanie's leg!

STEPHANIE: (Moans quietly) What, what, what are you going to do, Abby?

ABBY: Just stay still. I'm going to back up slowly. I need to find a long stick to use to distract the snake away from us. (Walks backward slowly. Searches alongside the path for a long, thick stick. Locates stick and picks it up.) This should work well. (Moves slowly back toward STEPHANIE) You're doing great, Stephanie. Now listen carefully to my plan.

Suddenly the snake begins to shake its rattles.

SEAN: Uh-oh. That doesn't sound good.

JESS: When they rattle like that, doesn't it mean they're upset and are thinking about biting?

ALEX: That's what I've heard. I wonder how Abby's going to help Stephanie.

STEPHANIE: (Whispering) Abby, why is the snake making that noise?

ABBY: That's its way of telling other living things that it's angry and scared. Listen to me carefully, Stephanie. It's very important that you do exactly as I say. When I tap you on the shoulder, I want you to very slowly move behind me. I'll hold out this stick as a target for the snake and gradually move in front of you to protect you. Do you understand my plan?

STEPHANIE: I think so, but I don't want you to get bit either.

ABBY: Don't worry about me. I've got this stick as a distraction. Let's do this!

ABBY gently taps STEPHANIE's shoulder. STEPHANIE slowly steps behind ABBY with small, careful movements, always keeping her eye on the snake. Meanwhile, ABBY holds the stick with a steady hand in front of the rattlesnake, as she takes small steps to move in front of STEPHANIE. When STEPHANIE is safely behind ABBY, ABBY shakes the stick at the snake. The snake strikes at the stick, then slithers quickly away into the woods. The other campers breathe a sigh of relief together.

JESS: Whoa! That was close!

STEPHANIE: (Trembling and hugging ABBY) Oh, Abby, thank you for protecting me. That was the scariest thing that ever happened to me.

ABBY: (Smiling in relief) That snake made my heart pound hard too. That's the closest I've ever been to a rattler!

SEAN: I hope it's the closest both of you will ever be again!

STEPHANIE: (Smiling at SEAN) No kidding!

ABBY: (Looks at her watch) Well, group, I think that's enough nature hiking for today. It will be lunch time soon. I don't know about you, but this excitement has made me work up an appetite. About a quarter of a mile up this trail is the main part of the camp. Let's walk quickly so we can be the first in line for lunch!

The group follows ABBY up the trail. As everyone passes the place where the snake slithered away, he or she nervously looks into the woods.

My *Life* in Jesus

Tell your classmates about a time when you were in danger and someone protected you. How was God active in this situation?

What are some ways that God protects you and cares for you daily?

Read the words of **1 Peter 5:7** from page 1. Why can we depend on God for care and protection?

The Second Article

[I believe] in Jesus Christ, His only Son, our Lord, who was conceived by the Holy Spirit, born of the Virgin Mary, suffered under Pontius Pilate, was crucified, died and was buried. He descended into hell. The third day He rose again from the dead. He ascended into heaven and sits at the right hand of God, the Father Almighty. From thence He will come to judge the living and the dead.

What does this mean? I believe that Jesus Christ, true God, begotten of the Father from eternity, and also true man, born of the Virgin Mary, is my Lord,

who has redeemed me, a lost and condemned person, purchased and won me from all sins, from death, and from the power of the devil; not with gold or silver, but with His holy, precious blood and with His innocent suffering and death,

that I may be His own and live under Him in His kingdom and serve Him in everlasting righteousness, innocence, and blessedness, just as He is risen from the dead, lives and reigns to all eternity. This is most certainly true.

Of whom does this article speak?

It speaks about Jesus Christ—His person and His work.

Why is He named *Jesus?*

Jesus means "the Lord saves." Jesus is His personal name.

Why is He called *Christ?*

The title *Christ* (Greek) or *Messiah* (Hebrew) means "the Anointed." Jesus has been anointed with the Holy Spirit without limit to be our Prophet, Priest, and King.

What does it mean when you confess, "I believe in Jesus Christ"?

It means that I trust in Jesus Christ as my only Savior from sin, death, and the devil and believe that He gives me eternal life.

Life Point

Christians believe that Jesus Christ is true God and true man.

My Life in Jesus Student Leaflets are published by Concordia Publishing House, 3558 S. Jefferson Ave., St. Louis, MO 63118-3968. Skit scripts written by Diane Grebing. Edited by Edward Grube. Scripture quotations: NIV®. Used by permission of Zondervan. All rights reserved. Catechism quotations: *Luther's Small Catechism with Explanation,* © 1986, 1991 CPH. Copyright © 2000 CPH. Printed in U.S.A. 22-2874

The Second Article—*Who Is Jesus?*

[Jesus] is the true God and eternal life. *1 John 5:20*

KARA, STEPHANIE, and JESS sit on ABBY's bunk inside their cabin as they look through a scrapbook.

Abby Revealed

KARA: (*Giggles*) Look at this picture of Abby in pigtails. I wonder if this was the first year she was at camp.

JESS: Why don't you just look at the caption under the picture, if you're so curious?

KARA: (*Looking intently at the page*) Oh, you're right, Jess. I see right here that it says, "First Year at Camp—1992."

STEPHANIE: (*Grabs for the book*) Hey, let me see that scrapbook. (*Thumbs through several pages and laughs*) Look at this one. It says, "Pie Eating Contest—1994. The blueberries were good, but messy!"

KARA and JESS look at the picture. Even JESS cracks a smile.

JESS: It probably took three days to get those blue stains off her cheeks.

STEPHANIE turns through three or four more pages of the scrapbook. Suddenly she stops, amazed.

STEPHANIE: Oh, wow, you guys! You should see these pages! There must be 20 swimming award ribbons on them.

JESS: Let me see that. (*Takes the scrapbook from STEPHANIE*) First Place, 100-meter butterfly; First Place, 200-meter backstroke; First Place, 100-meter free-style relay team; First Place, 200-meter free-style. She must have made first place in every event.

KARA: I had no idea Abby was such a great swimmer!

JESS: (*Turns another page in the book*) This is really something! Abby got a big certificate for getting a 100 percent on her lifesaving test. There's a little newspaper article next to the certificate. (*Scans the article*) It says here that less than one percent of all the people who take the lifesaving test get a perfect score.

STEPHANIE: That's really impressive! I remember last summer that a bunch of people were talking about what a strong swimmer she is. One of my friends even asked her about it. She didn't say anything about all these awards. (*Pauses*) You know, if I had won all those awards I'd sure let everyone know about it.

KARA: Maybe you would, Stephanie, but that's not the way Abby is. When you're as talented as she is, you don't need to tell everyone about it.

JESS: (*Thoughtfully*) I don't think it's just talent, Kara. Abby really cares about everything she does and everybody she meets.

STEPHANIE: I'm surprised to hear you say that, Jess! I thought you didn't like Abby at all.

JESS: (*Quietly*) I guess you don't know everything about me. I kind of admire her for sticking with me since I've been here. I'm not always the easiest person to get along with.

KARA: (*Proudly*) I think that's the best thing about Abby. She likes everyone and tries to treat everyone fairly. I'm really glad she's my counselor.

ABBY: (*From offstage*) Girls? Are you in the cabin?

STEPHANIE: Quick, Jess! Give me the scrapbook so I can put it away.

JESS hands STEPHANIE the scrapbook. STEPHANIE places it on the floor along the side of ABBY's bunk.

ABBY: (*ENTERS*) Well, there you all are! I've been looking all over for you. It's time for swimming, so get on your suits and we'll head down to the lake.

KARA: (*Waving her crutch*) Finally! Something I can do without this thing!

ABBY: (*Grinning*) T. J. was so excited when I told the boys we could swim that he almost ran down to the lake and jumped in with his clothes on.

JESS: (*With a big smile*) If that would have happened, you would have jumped right in to help him, right, Abby?

ABBY: I guess so. (*Looks at JESS for a moment*) You have a pretty smile, Jess. This is one of the first times I've seen it since camp started.

JESS: (*Shrugs her shoulders*) Let's not make a big deal out of it, okay?

ABBY: (*Curiously*) Okay. C'mon, girls, let's go! I hear the water's great!

ABBY EXITS as the girls eagerly follow.

My *Life* in Jesus

How did the girls' discoveries about Abby strengthen their relationship with her?

How does reading and studying the Bible strengthen your relationship with Jesus?

Share with your classmates at least one new truth you've learned concerning your life in Jesus since this course began.

The Second Article

[I believe] in Jesus Christ, His only Son, our Lord, who was conceived by the Holy Spirit, born of the Virgin Mary, suffered under Pontius Pilate, was crucified, died and was buried. He descended into hell. The third day He rose again from the dead. He ascended into heaven and sits at the right hand of God, the Father Almighty. From thence He will come to judge the living and the dead.

What does this mean? I believe that Jesus Christ, true God, begotten of the Father from eternity, and also true man, born of the Virgin Mary, is my Lord,

who has redeemed me, a lost and condemned person, purchased and won me from all sins, from death, and from the power of the devil; not with gold or silver, but with His holy, precious blood and with His innocent suffering and death,

that I may be His own and live under Him in His kingdom and serve Him in everlasting righteousness, innocence, and blessedness,

just as He is risen from the dead, lives and reigns to all eternity. This is most certainly true.

How has Christ rescued you from death? Through His suffering, death, and resurrection, Christ has triumphed over death. Since He now gives me eternal life I need not fear death.

How has Christ rescued you from the power of the devil? Christ has completely conquered the devil. Therefore the devil can no longer accuse me of my sins, and I can resist his temptations.

With what has Christ redeemed you? Christ has redeemed me, "not with gold or silver, but with His holy, precious blood and with His innocent suffering and death."

Life Point

Christians believe that Jesus came to rescue all people from sin and rose from the dead, giving all believers in Him the power to overcome sin and death forever.

MY LIFE IN JESUS STUDENT LEAFLETS are published by Concordia Publishing House, 3558 S. Jefferson Ave., St. Louis, MO 63118-3968. Skit scripts written by Diane Grebing. Edited by Edward Grube. Scripture quotations: NIV®. Used by permission of Zondervan. All rights reserved. Catechism quotations: *Luther's Small Catechism with Explanation,* © 1986, 1991 CPH. Copyright © 2000 CPH. Printed in U.S.A.   22-2874

[Jesus] died for all, that those who live should no longer live for themselves but for Him who died for them and was raised again.
2 Corinthians 5:15

ABBY, KARA, STEPHANIE, JESS, T. J., and SEAN are throwing a beach ball to one another in the swimming area of the lake. ALEX is swimming alone out in the deep end of the swimming area, close to the outer edge of the roped-off area.

The Rescue

ABBY: *(Holding the beach ball)* Hey, guys, now that we're used to the water, let's play water volleyball. *(Shades her eyes and looks out toward where ALEX is swimming)* Alex! You want to play volleyball with us?

ALEX: *(Looking back toward the others as he paddles along)* No thanks. I think I'll just swim out here for a while by myself.

ABBY: Okay, but be careful. You need to stay inside the ropes because there's a strong undertow just outside the swimming area.

ALEX: I'll be fine, because I'm a strong swimmer. Don't worry about me. *(Turns and continues to paddle)*

ABBY: Let's divide into two teams, three people on each side.

T. J.: How about Sean and me and Abby against you girls?

JESS: *(Taunts)* Even with Abby's help, you guys don't stand a chance!

ABBY: Let's move over here to the rope. *(The group swims over to the rope.)* We'll use this rope as the net. When the ball is served over to your side, it has to be hit by two different people before it can be returned to the other team. If the ball hits the water at any time, the team that is opposite of the side where the ball lands gets one point. The game ends when one team reaches 15 points. *(Holds the beach ball up to serve it)* Ready?

ABBY serves the ball. JESS hits it first, then KARA taps it over the rope to SEAN. SEAN taps the ball to T. J., who fumbles it. The ball hits the water.

T. J.: Sorry, guys. The sun was in my eyes.

JESS: *(Cheerfully)* One to nothing, our favor. It's our serve. Throw the ball over to me, would you, Abby?

ABBY looks out toward the end of the swimming area to spot ALEX.

ABBY: Did any of you notice if Alex swam into the shore?

SEAN: The last time I saw him he was over by the end of the rope.

The campers look out into the lake for ALEX. Suddenly his head bobs up out of the water, then goes back under.

T. J.: There he is, Abby. He's just bobbing up and down. He said he's a strong swimmer, so I'm sure he's fine. Let's get back to our game.

ABBY: *(Alarmed)* He's not fine, T. J. The undertow's got him.

ABBY furiously swims out to ALEX. The other campers watch in fear.

SEAN: What if Abby gets pulled down in the undertow too?

STEPHANIE: *(Trying to stay calm)* We saw Abby's scrapbook yesterday. She's won all kinds of swimming awards.

KARA: She got a 100 percent on her lifesaving test.

JESS: If anyone can help Alex, it's Abby.

The other campers continue to watch as ABBY swims out to ALEX, who continues to bob up and down.

ABBY: *(Breathlessly)* Alex! Alex! It's Abby. You're caught in the undertow. I'm going to put my arm around you. I want you to relax and lean back like you're doing the back float. I'll tow you to safety.

ALEX: I'm really scared, Abby! *(Pulls hard on ABBY's arm and brings her below the surface for a moment)*

T. J.: Oh, no, they're both down!

ABBY's head quickly bobs back up.

JESS: It's okay! Abby's back up!

KARA: Let's pray for God's help.

The campers join hands. JESS joins them at the last moment.

KARA: Dear God, please help Abby and Alex get back to the shore safely. Amen.

The campers look up to see ABBY slowly towing ALEX back toward shore.

SEAN: They're back inside the ropes!

STEPHANIE: *(Looking upward)* Thank You, God!

ABBY and ALEX near the shore. Finally they reach the beach. They both lie on the sand, exhausted. The other campers swim in quickly to join them.

T. J.: Alex, are you all right?

ALEX: *(Weakly)* Yeah, I think so. *(To ABBY)* I'm sorry. I thought I could swim out there. I guess I didn't understand the danger.

ABBY: *(Breathing heavily)* The important thing is you're okay.

My *Life* in Jesus

From what do all people need to be rescued? Does everyone always realize Satan's dangerous power? How has Jesus rescued us from eternal harm?

Recognizing the danger of sin, why is it important that we publicly confess our belief in Jesus and proclaim to others what He has done for us?

Read carefully "How has Christ rescued you from the power of the devil?" in the meaning of the Second Article on page 4. Because Jesus has rescued you from sin and eternal death, what are you now able to do?

The Third Article

I believe in the Holy Spirit, the holy Christian church, the communion of saints, the forgiveness of sins, the resurrection of the body, and the life everlasting. Amen.

What does this mean? I believe that I cannot by my own reason or strength believe in Jesus Christ, my Lord, or come to Him; but the Holy Spirit has called me by the Gospel, enlightened me with His gifts, sanctified and kept me in the true faith.

In the same way He calls, gathers, enlightens, and sanctifies the whole Christian church on earth, and keeps it with Jesus Christ in the one true faith.

In this Christian church He daily and richly forgives all my sins and the sins of all believers.

On the Last Day He will raise me and all the dead, and give eternal life to me and all believers in Christ.

This is most certainly true.

What is the special work of the Holy Spirit?

The Holy Spirit sanctifies me (makes me holy) by bringing me to faith in Christ, so that I might have the blessings of redemption and lead a godly life.

What has the Holy Spirit done to bring you to faith?

The Holy Spirit "has called me by the Gospel," that is, He has invited and drawn me by the Gospel to partake of the spiritual blessings that are mine in Christ.

What also does the Holy Spirit do for you?

The Holy Spirit by the Gospel keeps me in the true faith.

No one can say, "Jesus is Lord," except by the Holy Spirit.
1 Corinthians 12:3

Life Point

As Christians, we believe that the Holy Spirit brings us to faith in Jesus, keeps us in this true faith, and joins all believers together as the Christian church.

MY LIFE IN JESUS STUDENT LEAFLETS are published by Concordia Publishing House, 3558 S. Jefferson Ave., St. Louis, MO 63118-3968. Skit scripts written by Diane Grebing. Edited by Edward Grube. Scripture quotations: NIV®. Used by permission of Zondervan. All rights reserved. Catechism quotations: *Luther's Small Catechism with Explanation,* © 1986, 1991 CPH. Copyright © 2000 CPH. Printed in U.S.A. 22-2874

ABBY and THE CAMPERS are on the beach, still recovering after the rescue of ALEX from the deep water. JESS stands near ALEX while the other campers surround ABBY.

Visible Faith

JESS: That was scary! Alex, we thought you might drown.

ALEX: I thought I'd had it! Thank God Abby rescued me. There was no way I could have gotten out of that by myself.

JESS: I'm really glad that God was there to help you. Are you warm enough? Do you need another towel? Are you thirsty? I could get you some water.

ALEX: *(Gives a small laugh)* I think I've seen enough water for one day, thank you. *(Looks at JESS with a puzzled expression)* How come you're being so nice to me, anyway?

JESS: *(Shrugs her shoulders)* I don't know. Just feel like it, I guess.

ABBY comes over to ALEX and JESS.

ABBY: Thanks for being so kind and caring to Alex, Jess. It looks like the Holy Spirit's been working in your heart.

JESS: The Holy Spirit? Who's that?

ABBY: He's God. He puts faith in Jesus in our hearts, and He keeps us in that faith.

JESS: He's in my heart?

ABBY: *(Smiling)* Well, it's not like you can see Him with an X-ray! The Holy Spirit works in us as we hear God's Word, bringing us to faith. He keeps on working to help us show Jesus' love and care to others, just like your kindness to Alex.

The other campers come and stand around ALEX.

T. J.: *(Patting ALEX on the back)* You gave us quite a scare, man!

KARA: Can we do anything for you, Alex?

STEPHANIE: Could you use another towel?

SEAN: How about a snack?

ALEX: *(Grinning)* Enough, enough already! Thanks for all your concern, but I'm really fine.

JESS: *(Taps ABBY'S shoulder)* Is the Holy Spirit working in their hearts too?

ABBY: Yes, He is. The Holy Spirit brings all believers in Jesus together, keeps them in faith, and helps them show Jesus' love and care to each other as God's family, the church.

JESS: *(Ponders ABBY's comments)* Considering all that's happened today and how God answered Kara's prayer, I'd like to thank God.

ABBY: Why don't you say a prayer, Jess?

JESS: Pray out loud? I don't know how.

ABBY: That's another way the Holy Spirit works in our hearts. He helps us find the right words when we pray for others and when we witness to them about Jesus. Speak what's in your heart, Jess. The Holy Spirit will do the rest.

JESS: I guess I'll try.

ABBY: *(Gets the group's attention)* Listen, Jess wants to pray with you.

ABBY and THE CAMPERS fold their hands.

JESS: *(Hesitantly)* Thank You, God, for bringing Alex and Abby back safely to the shore. And, and thanks for everyone here who's been my friend. Amen. *(EXITS running)*

REMAINING CAMPERS look at each other, amazed.

T. J.: What was that all about?

SEAN: *(To ABBY)* How come Jess is running away?

ABBY: I think maybe Jess surprised herself today. The Holy Spirit's been working in her heart to help her. Let's give her a little space. *(Looks at her watch)* Anyway, we need to get back and get cleaned up for supper. I also heard a rumor that later tonight we're going to have a campfire and make s'mores.

ALEX: I'm glad I'm still here! I wouldn't want to miss s'mores.

ABBY: They're a camp tradition! Do you think you can make it back to the cabins okay, Alex?

ALEX: *(Slowly stands and takes a deep breath)* I think so.

T. J. and SEAN move to either side of ALEX.

SEAN: T. J. and I will be right by your side, if you need some help.

ALEX: *(Looking around at everyone)* Thanks, guys; especially you, Abby.

ALL EXIT together.

My *Life* in Jesus

What is the special work of the Holy Spirit?

Why do we need the Holy Spirit?

Name at least two ways that church families are meant to be blessings from God.

The Third Article

I believe in the Holy Spirit, the holy Christian church, the communion of saints, the forgiveness of sins, the resurrection of the body, and the life everlasting. Amen.

What does this mean? I believe that I cannot by my own reason or strength believe in Jesus Christ, my Lord, or come to Him; but the Holy Spirit has called me by the Gospel, enlightened me with His gifts, sanctified and kept me in the true faith.

In the same way He calls, gathers, enlightens, and sanctifies the whole Christian church on earth, and keeps it with Jesus Christ in the one true faith.

In this Christian church He daily and richly forgives all my sins and the sins of all believers.

On the Last Day He will raise me and all the dead, and give eternal life to me and all believers in Christ.

This is most certainly true.

How do you receive this forgiveness of sins?

Through faith, that is, by believing the Gospel.

To whom does God give eternal life?

God gives eternal life to me and all believers in Christ.
- Eternal life is a present possession.
- At the time of death, the soul of a believer is immediately with Christ in heaven.
- At the Last Day the believers, in both body and soul, will begin the full enjoyment of being with Christ forever.

Are you sure that you have eternal life?

Even as I now believe in Christ my Savior, I also know that I have been chosen to eternal life out of pure grace in Christ.

Life Point

Christians believe that God offers forgiveness in the Gospel, which proclaims salvation and eternal life through faith in Jesus Christ.

MY LIFE IN JESUS STUDENT LEAFLETS are published by Concordia Publishing House, 3558 S. Jefferson Ave., St. Louis, MO 63118-3968. Skit scripts written by Diane Grebing. Edited by Edward Grube. Scripture quotations: NIV®. Used by permission of Zondervan. All rights reserved. Catechism quotations: *Luther's Small Catechism with Explanation,* © 1986, 1991 CPH. Copyright © 2000 CPH. Printed in U.S.A. 22-2874

God so loved the world that He gave His one and only Son, that whoever believes in Him shall not perish but have eternal life.
John 3:16

THE CAMPERS are sitting around a campfire with ABBY in the late evening SEAN and T. J. are roasting marshmallows on long sticks. KARA, JESS, and STEPHANIE are eating s'mores. ALEX is sitting quietly beside ABBY.

What If ... ?

STEPHANIE: *(Munching happily)* I think these s'mores are even better than the ones we made last summer.

ABBY: It's the giant marshmallows I use. It makes them nice and gooey.

T. J.: *(Pointing)* Hey Sean, your marshmallow's on fire!

SEAN: *(Rapidly pulls his stick out of the fire and blows on the glowing marshmallow)* Thanks, T. J. That one was almost toast!

ALEX: *(Tensely)* It's just a stupid marshmallow, guys. There's a lot bigger things in life to worry about.

T. J.: *(To ALEX)* What's eating you?

ALEX: *(Angrily)* Nothing. I just can't believe how somebody can get so bent out of shape over something like marshmallows when in the next minute you could be dead.

The group stares at ALEX.

ABBY: *(Quietly)* You've had a pretty upsetting day, haven't you, Alex?

ALEX: *(Nods yes)* When I was out there caught in the undertow and realized I couldn't save myself, I wondered about what it would be like to die and what would happen to me.

KARA: I wondered about that too, Alex, when I had my knee surgery. I worried I might not wake up from the anesthesia.

JESS: *(Boldly)* I'm not afraid to admit it. I'm scared to die.

T. J. and SEAN slowly nod in agreement.

STEPHANIE: I sometimes worry about when I die that maybe I won't go to heaven because I've done something that God won't forgive.

ABBY: You've raised some interesting questions that a lot of other people think about too. But let me tell you some really Good News that helps when you have doubts, worries, and questions like these. You can believe God forgives your sins because, through Jesus, God has declared forgiveness to all sinners. Because Jesus died for our sins, God no longer holds our sins against us. All our sins were charged against Jesus, who paid for them with His life.

JESS: But how do we know for *sure* that we have God's forgiveness?

ABBY: The Gospel—God's Good News for us in Jesus—says so. The Holy Spirit gives us faith to believe the Gospel. He assures us that God will forgive our sins.

SEAN: Doesn't it say in the Bible that nothing can separate us from God's love in Jesus?

ABBY: That's one of my favorite verses, Sean. Not even death can keep us from Jesus.

ALEX: Then I guess I don't have enough faith, because I was scared to die today.

ABBY: Death can be frightening. But just as we can rely on God's promise to forgive our sins, we can also rely on His promise that says whoever believes in Jesus will not perish but have eternal life (John 3:16). Our bodies may die, but our souls will live forever.

KARA: Before I had my knee surgery, my pastor visited me in the hospital. I told him I was afraid I wouldn't wake up. He reminded me that Jesus promised He would be with us always. After I thought about that for a while, I realized that even if I didn't wake up from the surgery, I'd actually be better than okay. I would be with Jesus in heaven.

STEPHANIE: My favorite Bible verse is John 10:27–28: "My sheep listen to My voice; I know them, and they follow Me. I give them eternal life, and they shall never perish; no one can snatch them out of My hand." When I feel afraid or worried, I remember this verse.

ABBY: God gives us all these great promises in His Word to help us when we face frightening situations. God's Word is true, and the Holy Spirit gives us faith to trust in all of God's promises.

JESS: If only our souls go to heaven, what happens to our bodies?

ABBY: The Bible tells us that when Jesus returns to earth, we will rise physically from the dead. God will make our bodies to be perfect and they will last forever. We don't know exactly what they will be like, but if they are from God, we can trust that they will be really wonderful.

T. J.: *(Pointing)* Uh-oh, Abby. There goes *your* marshmallow.

ABBY: *(Winks at ALEX)* Oh, it's just a marshmallow; right, Alex?

My *Life* in Jesus

What are some worries and doubts people your age have about their faith?

What causes such doubts?

How can remembering God's promises concerning forgiveness of sins and eternal life help you when you have worries?

Share with your classmates a promise of God that helps you when you have problems and worries.

The Introduction to the Lord's Prayer:

- Our Father who art in heaven.
  What does this mean? With these words God tenderly invites us to believe that He is our true Father and that we are His true children, so that with all boldness and confidence we may ask Him as dear children ask their dear Father.

In what way does the word *Father* in the Lord's Prayer encourage us to pray?

The word *Father* tells us that God loves us and wants us to pray to Him confidently and without fear.

What does the word *our* impress upon us when we pray, "Our Father"?

In Jesus all believers are children of the one Father and should pray with and for one another.

What do the words *who art [are] in heaven* say about God?

These words assure us that our heavenly Father, as Lord over all, has the power to grant our prayers.

The First Petition

- Hallowed be Thy name.
  What does this mean? God's name is certainly holy in itself, but we pray in this petition that it may be kept holy among us also.
  How is God's name kept holy? God's name is kept holy when the Word of God is taught in its truth and purity, and we, as the children of God, also lead holy lives according to it. Help us to do this, dear Father in heaven! But anyone who teaches or lives contrary to God's Word profanes the name of God among us. Protect us from this, heavenly Father!

Life Point

God our Heavenly Father invites us to pray to Him and hears and answers all our prayers for Jesus' sake.

MY LIFE IN JESUS STUDENT LEAFLETS are published by Concordia Publishing House, 3558 S. Jefferson Ave., St. Louis, MO 63118-3968. Skit scripts written by Diane Grebing. Edited by Edward Grube. Scripture quotations: NIV®. Used by permission of Zondervan. All rights reserved. Catechism quotations: *Luther's Small Catechism with Explanation*, © 1986, 1991 CPH. Copyright © 2000 CPH. Printed in U.S.A.

22-2874

How great is the love the Father has lavished on us, that we should be called children of God! And that is what we are! *1 John 3:1*

The campers stand outside the mess hall. ABBY is holding a letter and a small box wrapped in brown paper. KARA, T. J., ALEX, SEAN, and STEPHANIE wait eagerly to see who received mail. JESS stands toward the back of the group with a distressed expression.

You've Got Mail

ABBY: Mail call! We've really got a pile of letters today!

KARA: I can't wait to see if my mom wrote me a letter. She promised she'd let me know how my sister Sharon did at her swim meet. Did I tell you guys she's one of the fastest swimmers for her age?

T. J.: Maybe she could come and show Alex a thing or two!

STEPHANIE: I hope my mom sent me a picture of the house she and my dad are thinking about buying. It would be great to move out of our apartment and have a place with a backyard.

ABBY: Let's see, Stephanie, here's a letter for you. *(Gives the letter to STEPHANIE)* T. J., Alex, Kara, Sean, and Jess, here are your letters.

ABBY distributes the mail to SEAN, T. J., ALEX, STEPHANIE, and KARA, who then EXIT. JESS steps forward last, reluctantly taking hers.

ABBY: *(Quietly to JESS)* Jess, is something wrong?

JESS: When you had us write home a few days ago, I put some things in my letter that maybe I shouldn't have. I told my parents how upset I was that they sent me off to camp and how I was lonely for them. I don't know how they'll take it. *(Jams the unopened letter in her pocket)*

ABBY: You'll never know how they feel if you don't read the letter.

JESS: I'll read it later—after I've gathered up some courage. *(Looking with interest at ABBY's package)* Boy, you must rate! You got a package!

ABBY: Oh, that's my dad. I love opening his packages because I never quite know what I'll find in them. Want to open it with me?

ABBY and JESS sit down on a bench. ABBY opens the package.

ABBY: *(Chuckles)* I can't believe he sent me this!

JESS: *(Peers in the box)* A stuffed rabbit? Why would he send you this?

ABBY: That's not just a old stuffed rabbit. That's Mr. Cottonball. I've had him since I was three years old. My dad brought him home one day when I wasn't feeling well. I've kept it all these years because it reminds me of the kindness and care my dad always shows me. *(Takes the rabbit out of the box and notices a note under it. Takes out the note and opens it.)* Here's a note. It says, "Dear Abby, Mr. Cottonball missed you. So do I. I've been thinking of you often. Hope you're having fun at camp. Love, Dad."

JESS: Aren't you kind of old to have your dad think about you all the time?

ABBY: I don't think I'll ever grow too old to have my dad think about me. That's the way it is with my dad. He always cares about me and my family. I know I can always come to him, even now that I'm older. He always listens to me and helps me.

JESS: I wish I had a dad like that.

ABBY: *(Smiling)* You do, Jess.

JESS: Look, Abby, neither my mom nor dad care about me.

ABBY: I'm talking about your heavenly Father, Jess—God. Through our faith in Jesus, we're all God's children. God your Father loves you so much. He always wants to hear from you. He promises to listen and to help you always, no matter how old you get.

JESS: It's really hard to figure out what to say to God, especially when it's something about me. He's got so many people to think about. I don't need to bother Him with my little problems.

ABBY: None of our problems are little to God, Jess. And our prayers don't have to be said out loud. We can talk to God silently in our thoughts. *(Pauses)* I sometimes have trouble, too, knowing what to say when I pray. But then I remember the beginning words of the Lord's Prayer, the prayer Jesus gave us. Have you heard them?

JESS: Isn't that the prayer people say at church, the one that starts out with something about "Father"?

ABBY: That's right. The Lord's Prayer begins, "Our Father who art in heaven." The word *Father* tells us a lot about the relationship we have with God. He loves us in the best way that a Father can love a child.

JESS: Would God help me with this problem with my parents?

ABBY: I know He will! Your heavenly Fathers hears all your prayers and answers them in the way that is best for you.

JESS: *(Reaches for the letter in her back pocket)* If it's okay with you, I think I'd like to be alone for a while. I'll ask God to be with me when I read my letter from home. Since you say I'm His child, maybe He will see things from my point of view. *(Walks away from ABBY; EXITS)*

My *Life* in Jesus

Based on what Abby told Jess, define prayer.

How does knowing that God is your *Father* affect your prayers?

Are there right and wrong ways to pray? Explain your answer.

The Second Petition

Thy kingdom come.

What does this mean? The kingdom of God certainly comes by itself without our prayer, but we pray in this petition that it may come to us also.

How does God's kingdom come? God's kingdom comes when our heavenly Father gives us His Holy Spirit, so that by His grace we believe His holy Word and lead godly lives here in time and there in eternity.

What is the kingdom of God?

The kingdom of God is His ruling as king over the whole universe (kingdom of power), the church on earth (kingdom of grace), and the church and angels in heaven (kingdom of glory).

For what do we pray in the Second Petition?

We do not pray that God's kingdom of power would come, because that is already present everywhere, but we ask God to

- give us His Holy Spirit so that we believe His Word and lead godly lives as members of His kingdom of grace;
- bring many others into His kingdom of grace;
- use us to extend His kingdom of grace;
- hasten the coming of His kingdom of glory.

Life Point

We pray, as members of God's kingdom through faith in Jesus, that all people come to faith in Him.

MY LIFE IN JESUS STUDENT LEAFLETS are published by Concordia Publishing House, 3558 S. Jefferson Ave., St. Louis, MO 63118-3968. Skit scripts written by Diane Grebing. Edited by Edward Grube. Scripture quotations: NIV®. Used by permission of Zondervan. All rights reserved. Catechism quotations: *Luther's Small Catechism with Explanation,* © 1986, 1991 CPH. Copyright © 2000 CPH. Printed in U.S.A.

22-2874

He has rescued us from the dominion of darkness and brought us into the kingdom of the Son He loves, in whom we have redemption, the forgiveness of sins. *Colossians 1:13–14*

ALEX, STEPHANIE, T. J., KARA, and SEAN gather at a table in the recreation building as they work on a craft project with beads and lanyard cord. Suddenly JESS enters the building. She walks past ABBY and throws a crumpled letter on the table.

God's Kingdom for Jesus

JESS: I thought you said that God is on my side and that He would see things from my point of view!

ABBY: Calm down, Jess. God *is* on your side. He loves you and cares for you and wants you in His kingdom.

JESS: You're wrong! If God loves me so much, then why did He let this happen to me? *(Points angrily at the crumpled letter)*

ABBY: *(Gently)* What did your parents say, Jess?

JESS: Oh, they said plenty of things! Their main point was if I feel so neglected at home, they would be happy to make arrangements so I would never have to go back there.

KARA: *(Horrified)* Jess, that's awful! That's really what they said?

JESS: *(Picks up the letter and gives it to KARA)* Here! Read it yourself. Page 2, paragraph 3.

KARA: *(Uncrumples the letter, scans the page and reads aloud)* "We're sorry, Jess, that you think we don't care about you. If you would be happier not living with us, we can check with your grandparents in Lockwood. Maybe you can stay with them."

T. J.: *(Cautiously)* That doesn't exactly sound to me like they don't want you, Jess.

JESS: *(Angrily)* What do you know? You've got a family who loves you. I don't have a family anywhere.

STEPHANIE: Yes you do, Jess.

JESS: *(Sarcastically)* Oh, so you're planning on calling your happy little family to see if they'll take me in! Let me tell you, it will never happen. Your parents will take one look at me and decide they don't want me either.

STEPHANIE: That's not what I meant, Jess. I was talking about God's family. Everyone who believes in Jesus is part of it.

JESS: Look, I already tried trusting in God once. Abby told me all about how He is my loving heavenly Father. Well, if He cares about me so much, He sure has a strange way of showing it.

ABBY: God does love you, Jess. He's sorry that you're hurting right now. Sometimes we don't understand why certain things happen. But God can work good for us in all things.

JESS: So now you're saying that my parents not wanting me is a good thing? If that's God's idea of good, I say, "No thanks!" *(EXITS, sobbing)*

ALEX: She's really upset now.

SEAN: *(Turns to ABBY)* Can't you do something to help her?

ABBY: Ever since we've been at camp, I've been praying for God to help Jess with her family problems and with all her anger. She's really hurting inside and feels like she doesn't belong anywhere. She's so upset right now that she won't take anything we say the right way. *(Pauses)* I think God has given all of us a challenge here. He wants us to show Jess His love and care. God wants to use us to show Jess His goodness and His wonderful grace for her in Jesus.

T. J.: But you just said Jess is not listening to anybody. If God hasn't answered your prayers about her yet, how is He going to help her through us now?

ABBY: I don't know, T. J., but I do know that since He loved us so much to send our Savior, we can count on Him to help us find a way to help Jess.

KARA: Let's ask God again for His help. *(THE CAMPERS and ABBY bow their heads.)* Dear Father, You know we're worried about Jess. We want to help her. Please show us the right things to do so that she will see Your love and care for her. In Jesus' name we pray. Amen.

STEPHANIE: Don't you think we better look for Jess?

ABBY: Of course! Alex, T. J., and Sean, go check for Jess down by the lake. Kara, you check our cabin. Stephanie, look over by the mess hall while I check the hiking trail. *(Looks at her watch)* Meet me back here in 10 minutes, and if you find Jess, bring her with you.

ALL EXIT.

My *Life* in Jesus

Read carefully the words of Colossians 1:13–14 from page 1. How is your life different as a member of God's kingdom?

God is in control because His kingdom of power is present everywhere. How does that change our outlook when we face difficult situations? (See Psalm 50:15.)

How can you show and share the benefits of kingdom living with others, like Jess, who may be unhappy?

The Third Petition

Thy will be done on earth as it is in heaven.

What does this mean? The good and gracious will of God is done even without our prayer, but we pray in this petition that it may be done among us also.

How is God's will done? God's will is done when He breaks and hinders every evil plan and purpose of the devil, the world, and our sinful nature, which do not want us to hallow God's name or let His kingdom come;

and when He strengthens and keeps us firm in His Word and faith until we die.

This is His good and gracious will.

What is the good and gracious will of God?

It is God's will that His name be kept holy and that His kingdom come, that is, that His Word be taught correctly and that sinners be brought to faith in Christ and lead godly lives.

How is God's will done in our lives?

God's will is done when

- He breaks and hinders the plans of the devil, the world, and our sinful nature, which try to destroy our faith in Christ Jesus;
- He strengthens and keeps us firm in His Word and faith and helps us lead God-pleasing lives;
- He supports us in all our troubles until we die.

Life Point

We can confidently pray, "Thy will be done," knowing that God works good for all who believe in Him.

MY LIFE IN JESUS STUDENT LEAFLETS are published by Concordia Publishing House, 3558 S. Jefferson Ave., St. Louis, MO 63118-3968. Skit scripts written by Diane Grebing. Edited by Edward Grube. Scripture quotations: NIV®. Used by permission of Zondervan. All rights reserved. Catechism quotations: *Luther's Small Catechism with Explanation,* © 1986, 1991 CPH. Copyright © 2000 CPH. Printed in U.S.A.   22-2874

We know that in all things God works for the good of those who love Him, who have been called according to His purpose.
Romans 8:28

ABBY, SEAN, STEPHANIE, ALEX, and *T. J. stand at the entrance to the recreation building.*

Prayer Warriors

SEAN: I didn't see Jess anywhere.

ALEX: Do you think she ran away?

T. J.: Once, I saw this TV show about a runaway …

ABBY: That's enough, T. J. I checked the entire trail, and Stephanie searched the mess hall. Even though we didn't find Jess, I don't think she ran away.

STEPHANIE: Maybe Kara saw her.

KARA ENTERS, hobbling on her crutch; JESS ENTERS at her side.

ABBY: *(Hurries over to KARA and JESS)* Jess, I'm so glad Kara found you!

JESS: *(Mumbling)* I need to leave. I'll just call my grandparents and see if they can pick me up.

SEAN: But we don't want you to go! You're part of our group.

JESS: Why not? Why should I stick around here? In a few days, camp will be over. A day or two after that, you guys will forget all about me, just like God has.

T. J.: God doesn't forget about anyone, Jess.

JESS: If that's true, then why doesn't He help me with my parents?

ABBY: God always hears us when we pray to Him, Jess. He's in control of every situation, even though it may not seem like it. God promises that in all things He works for our good.

JESS: Do you think that what's happening to me is good?

ABBY: Of course not, Jess. But God can make good things happen for us even through bad situations.

KARA: When I hurt my knee, I thought, "How could God let this happen to me? He knows how much I love to play softball in the summer. He knows that I was coming to camp." I was really upset. Satan loves it when we get that way, because he tries to use those feelings to turn us away from God. It's been hard having to use a crutch all these weeks, especially here. But God is helping my knee to heal. I still got to go to camp. *(Gestures around the group)* I've met all of you. I've also learned some patience, especially for other people who have physical problems and can't move very quickly.

SEAN: Satan uses all kinds of things to make us doubt God's care for us. In situations that are especially hard on us, like the kind you're going through with your parents, Satan works twice as hard. First, he wants us to think the problem is God's idea. Second, he wants us to think that God doesn't care when we're worried or hurt or afraid. Sin and hurtful things in the world are not God's idea. Satan tricks us into thinking that God causes bad things. In reality, it's our own sinfulness and the devil's work that causes them.

ALEX: It's a battle, Jess. Lots of us have tough problems. We can depend on God to help us. After all, He already helped us with our toughest problem, our sins, by sending Jesus to die on the cross. Satan won't admit it now, but Jesus already overcame him and all evil when He rose from the dead.

ABBY: *(Amazed at the insights)* They're right, Jess. God's will for you is to keep you close to Him and to protect you from Satan's evil attacks. God wants to help you with your problem.

T. J.: I know I've teased you before, Jess, but I really do care about you. At my church, when people have problems, we pray with them. We've prayed *for* you already. I think it's time we pray *with* you.

ABBY: That's a great idea, T. J. Jess, what do you think?

JESS: *(Embarrassed)* I didn't think my problem mattered to you.

STEPHANIE: *(Walks over to JESS and stands beside her)* It does, Jess.

ABBY: Let's pray.

ALL gather together in a circle. They fold their hands and bow their heads.

ABBY: Heavenly Father, You made the world and You control it. We can be sure You want the best for us because You sent Jesus, Your Son, to be our Savior. You know that Jess is having a hard time with her family. Work in all their hearts, Lord, so they will know Your love and kindness. Help them show this love and kindness to each other. Help Jess to trust in You and in Your will for her. In Jesus' name we pray. Amen.

JESS: I've never had people pray for me before. At least now I don't feel so alone.

My *Life* in Jesus

How does Satan try to attack God's people?

How does reading and studying God's Word help us remain strong when we face troubles?

When friends face difficult situations, what are some specific requests you can make to God as you pray for them?

God's will is done even without our prayers. Why is this a comfort? Why do we still pray that God's will is done in our lives?

The Fourth Petition

Give us this day our daily bread.

What does this mean? God certainly gives daily bread to everyone without our prayers, even to all evil people, but we pray in this petition that God would lead us to realize this and to receive our daily bread with thanksgiving.

What is meant by daily bread? Daily bread includes everything that has to do with the support and needs of the body, such as food, drink, clothing, shoes, house, home, land, animals, money, goods, a devout husband or wife, devout children, devout workers, devout and faithful rulers, good government, good weather, peace, health, self-control, good reputation, good friends, faithful neighbors and the like.

Why do we pray to God for daily bread?

We pray to God for daily bread, which includes everything that has to do with the support and needs of the body, because Christ wants us to

- realize that our entire life and that of everyone else depends on God;
- receive all our physical blessings with thanksgiving;
- look to God for physical as well as spiritual blessings.

What does God want us to do for those who are unable to work for daily food?

God does not want us to be selfish but to share with those who are unable to work and to include them in our prayers for daily bread.

Why does Jesus have us say "this day" and "daily"?

These words teach us not to be greedy or wasteful or to worry about the future but to live contentedly in the confidence that the Lord will give us what we need.

Life Point

In prayer, we can confidently ask God to provide for our daily needs and trust that He will do it.

MY LIFE IN JESUS STUDENT LEAFLETS are published by Concordia Publishing House, 3558 S. Jefferson Ave., St. Louis, MO 63118-3968. Skit scripts written by Diane Grebing. Edited by Edward Grube. Scripture quotations: NIV®. Used by permission of Zondervan. All rights reserved. Catechism quotations: *Luther's Small Catechism with Explanation*, © 1986, 1991 CPH. Copyright © 2000 CPH. Printed in U.S.A.

The eyes of all look to You, and You give them their food at the proper time. You open Your hand and satisfy the desires of every living thing.
Psalm 145:15–16

CAMP WONDERMENT

ABBY and THE CAMPERS are hiking the road just outside of the Camp Wonderment entrance. As they hike, they notice a number of torn and empty food containers.

CONCORDIA COLLEGE LIBRARY
BRONXVILLE, NEW YORK 10708

Sharing Daily Bread

T. J.: I can't believe what slobs people can be! *(Points at litter)* It looks like someone drove by and tossed garbage out the car window.

ALEX: *(Stoops to pick up a torn and chewed-on cereal box)* This group must have come from some family with really big teeth. Look at the bite marks on the side of this box! *(Shows box to the others)*

ABBY: Let me see that for a moment, Alex. *(Takes the box from ALEX and examines it carefully)* These are not human teeth marks, guys. This is the work of a bear.

STEPHANIE: *(Startled)* A bear! Around here?

SEAN: It's certainly not impossible. Camp Wonderment is surrounded by national forest. I've read that several black bears were sighted in this area over the past few summers.

ABBY: That's right, Sean. Even though there's lots for the bears to eat in the forest, when they smell human food, they go right after it.

KARA: When my family drove me up here, I noticed that there's a park campground about a mile up the road.

ABBY: That campground has been a part of the national forest for a lot longer than Camp Wonderment's been here. I've heard it's a really nice campground, if you enjoy tent camping.

The sound of crackling branches is heard from behind THE CAMPERS. The group turns around quickly.

STEPHANIE: Did you guys hear that? Maybe that bear is close by.

ABBY: Just to be on the safe side, I want you guys to get behind me. Stay right here while I check this out.

ABBY tiptoes toward the sound. Suddenly, JAY steps out from the bushes.

ABBY: Why, hello there!

JESS: We sure are glad you're not a bear!

JAY: Sorry if I startled you. My name's Jay Turner. As for that bear, I'd like to get my hands on it right about now. My wife and I have been camping over in the national forest. While we were out hiking, it got into our food supply. A week's worth of meals are scattered from here all the way back to our tent.

ABBY: Once those bears find human food, they can be pretty big pigs.

ALEX: *(Holds up the torn box)* I don't think you'll be having cereal for breakfast anytime soon.

JAY: The worst thing is that my in-laws dropped my wife and me off with our supplies. The nearest grocery store is about 20 miles away. There's no way we could hike that far and then carry six-days' worth of groceries all the way back.

T. J.: Can we help them, Abby? The mess hall is full of food. I bet they'd have enough for Jay and his wife for the rest of their camping trip.

SEAN: I've got lots of granola bars that I brought from home. I'd be happy to share them with you.

STEPHANIE: My mom sent all kinds of trail mix with me. I'll never be able to eat it all. You and your wife are welcome to share it, Jay.

JAY: *(Smiles)* I can't get over your generosity. As I walked along searching for any food the bear might have missed, I asked God to help me get some new supplies. My wife and I planned this trip for many months. We sure would be disappointed if we had to end it early. I can't believe how quickly God answered my prayers through your help!

ABBY: God finds many ways to provide for our needs. I know we can find you and your wife plenty to eat at the mess hall. Why don't you meet us there for lunch at a quarter to 12? That will give us some time to box up some food that you can take back to your campsite.

T. J.: We'll be sure to pack it up in some bear-proof containers!

JAY: *(Chuckles)* That's great! *(Checks his watch)* I'll head back to the campground to get my wife. We'll see you later. *(EXITS)*

ABBY: We'd better get over to the mess hall, gang, to alert the cooks that we need some food gathered together.

JESS: God sure answered Jay's prayer quickly.

ABBY: God knows all our needs and uses many different ways and people to provide for them.

JESS: Maybe there's hope for me yet.

ABBY: There's always hope in the Lord, Jess.

My *Life* in Jesus

Think about the hours you have spent since you got out of bed today. Share with your group at least three ways God has met your needs so far.

Why do you think we sometimes forget God's daily provisions for us? What are some things you can do to remember and thank God for these daily gifts?

In the Lord's Prayer, we pray, "Give us this *day* our *daily* bread." Why do we ask God to meet our needs on a daily basis?

The Lord's Prayer: The Fifth Petition—
Why Should We Forgive Others?

21

The Fifth Petition

And forgive us our trespasses as we forgive those who trespass against us.

What does this mean? We pray in this petition that our Father in heaven would not look at our sins, or deny our prayer because of them. We are neither worthy of the things for which we pray, nor have we deserved them, but we ask that He would give them all to us by grace, for we daily sin much and surely deserve nothing but punishment. So we too will sincerely forgive and gladly do good to those who sin against us.

What do we ask for in this petition?

We ask that our Father in heaven would for Christ's sake graciously forgive our sins.

Why do we include a prayer for forgiveness of sins in these petitions to our heavenly Father?

We are not worthy of the things for which we pray and have not deserved them. We therefore need God's forgiveness so that we may pray to Him confidently and in good conscience.

What does God want us to do for those who sin against us?

Our heavenly Father wants us to forgive and to do good to those who sin against us.

What does it show when we forgive others?

It shows that we truly believe that God has forgiven us.

Life Point

As forgiven sinners through faith in Jesus, our Savior, we pray for God's help so that we may forgive others who sin against us.

MY LIFE IN JESUS STUDENT LEAFLETS are published by Concordia Publishing House, 3558 S. Jefferson Ave., St. Louis, MO 63118-3968. Skit scripts written by Diane Grebing. Edited by Edward Grube. Scripture quotations: NIV®. Used by permission of Zondervan. All rights reserved. Catechism quotations: *Luther's Small Catechism with Explanation,* © 1986, 1991 CPH. Copyright © 2000 CPH. Printed in U.S.A.

22-2874

Be kind and compassionate to one another, forgiving each other, just as in Christ God forgave you. *Ephesians 4:32*

T. J., SEAN, and ALEX are sitting around on their bunks in their cabin. ABBY pokes her head in the window.

A Doodle of a Situation

ABBY: Good grief! This place is a mess!

T. J.: *(Grinning)* We're trying to win the messiest cabin award.

ABBY: *(Holding her nose)* I think you're on track to be double winners—the messiest and the smelliest!

SEAN: That's probably T. J.'s wet cheese doodles you smell.

ABBY: T. J.'s what?

SEAN: T. J.'s wet cheese doodles. A few nights ago, we were trying to see who could stick the most cheese doodles to the window, and …

ALEX: Quiet Sean, or we'll really be in trouble.

ABBY: I think I've heard enough. Whose turn is it to clean the cabin?

ALEX: Not mine. I cleaned it three days ago.

SEAN: I did it the time before that.

ALEX, SEAN, and ABBY stare at T. J.

T. J.: *(Reluctantly)* I guess it's my turn.

ABBY: Thank you, T. J. I'll come back in two hours to check your work. That should give you plenty of time to clean things up. *(EXITS)*

T. J.: *(Slowly picks up some clothes off the floor)* Man, she's worse than my mom. She's always nagging me to clean up my room at home.

ALEX: I can see why, especially if it looks anything like this place!

T. J.: *(Throws the clothes on the floor in exasperation)* I'm supposed to be here to have fun. *(Looks at his watch)* It's free time until three o'clock. I'm going swimming until a quarter to. Then I'll come back and straighten things up. Fifteen minutes should give me plenty of time.

SEAN: That kind of cuts it close, doesn't it, T. J.? I thought that's when Abby said she'd be back.

T. J.: You worry too much, Sean. *(Grabs his towel)* C'mon, guys! I'll race you down to the lake. *(BOYS EXIT)*

ABBY ENTERS, walks back toward the boys' cabin.

ABBY: *(Looks at her watch)* Well, it's three o'clock. T. J. should have the place all cleaned up by now. *(Opens the cabin door and peers inside)* I don't believe it! T. J. hasn't cleaned up one thing! *(Walks into the cabin and over to the window)* Oh, no! This window sill is crawling with ants! It must be the cheese doodles that are attracting them. I need to get some paper towels to clean this up. *(EXITS running)*

T. J. ENTERS. He quickly starts to stuff things under his bunk.

ABBY: *(ENTERS cabin with paper towels in hand)* Well, T. J., I see you finally got around to doing what I asked you to do two hours ago.

T. J.: *(Turns around to face ABBY)* Uh-oh!

ABBY: *(Firmly)* "Uh-oh" is right! Check the window sill, would you please?

T. J. walks over to the window sill.

T. J.: Oh, man, it's covered with ants! *(Begins bashing them with his fist, then turns and looks sheepishly at ABBY)* The cheese doodles, right?

ABBY: *(Walks over to T. J.)* Here. Use these. *(Hands T. J. the paper towels)*

T. J.: *(Wipes up the ants)* Thanks, Abby. I'm sorry about the ants.

ABBY: I am too, T. J. A few more hours and they would have been all over the bunks. But that's not what's making me the most upset.

T. J.: *(Looks around ashamed)* I didn't do my job very well, did I?

ABBY: You didn't do your job at all. It's bad enough that you let things get this messy in the first place. What really upsets me is that you promised to do something important and you didn't follow through.

T. J.: I'm sorry about the mess. *(Pauses)* I'm also sorry I disappointed you.

ABBY: *(Patiently)* We all disobey, T. J., sometimes by what we do, sometimes by not doing what we should. I forgive you. I know you recognize how you disobeyed, and I trust that you'll fix it.

T. J. nods yes. ALEX and SEAN enter the cabin.

ALEX: Uh-oh, T. J.! It looks like you got busted!

ABBY: That's true, Alex, but for Jesus' sake, God forgives us, fixes our "busted" relationships, and helps us do things that please Him.

T. J.: Thanks, Abby. I'll have this place cleaned up in no time!

ABBY: I know you will, T. J. See you guys later. *(EXITS)*

SEAN: *(Lies on his bunk and points at the floor)* Hey, you missed a spot!

ALEX: I'd watch it if I were you, Sean. T. J. will cheese-doodle you!

T. J.: *(Laughs)* My cheese doodle days are over, guys.

My Life in Jesus

In what ways did T. J. sin?

What consequences do our sins of action and inaction have?

How did Abby mirror God's forgiveness toward T. J.?

Knowing God in Christ completely forgives us, how are we freed to act toward others when they sin against us?

No temptation has seized you except what is common to man. And God is faithful; … when you are tempted, He will also provide a way out.
1 Corinthians 10:12–13

The Sixth Petition

And lead us not into temptation.

What does this mean? God tempts no one. We pray in this petition that God would guard and keep us so that the devil, the world, and our sinful nature may not deceive us or mislead us into false belief, despair, and other great shame and vice. Although we are attacked by these things, we pray that we may finally overcome them and win the victory.

What do *tempt* and *temptation* mean in the Scriptures?

In the Scriptures these words have two meanings:
- The testing of our faith, which God uses to bring us closer to Himself.
- The attempts of our spiritual enemies to lure us away from God and His ways.

What do we ask God to do for us when we pray this petition?

We ask our Father in heaven to give us strength to resist and overcome temptations.

REC ROOM

Life Point

We pray, asking God to give us strength to resist and overcome all temptation through Jesus' victory on the cross.

MY LIFE IN JESUS STUDENT LEAFLETS are published by Concordia Publishing House, 3558 S. Jefferson Ave., St. Louis, MO 63118-3968. Skit scripts written by Diane Grebing. Edited by Edward Grube. Scripture quotations: NIV®. Used by permission of Zondervan. All rights reserved. Catechism quotations: *Luther's Small Catechism with Explanation*, © 1986, 1991 CPH. Copyright © 2000 CPH. Printed in U.S.A.

22-2874

T. J., SEAN, ALEX, STEPHANIE, KARA, and JESS sit around a table inside the recreation building. All are bored and mopey because it is pouring down rain outside.

Tempted

ABBY: How about a checker tournament?

T. J.: Checkers? The last time I played that game I was five years old.

ABBY: How about the rest of you? Kara? Stephanie?

STEPHANIE: I don't know. Checkers doesn't seem like much fun to me.

ABBY: Well, let's make things interesting. Why don't the six of you play between yourselves. Then the winner will play me. What do you say?

ALEX: *(Suddenly interested)* Do we get anything if we win?

ABBY: *(Thinks)* Well, I happen to know where the cooks keep some frozen pizzas. How about all the pizza you can eat?

T. J.: I'm in! Even though the food in the mess hall is okay, I've about had my fill of beanie weenies. A pizza would hit the spot.

ABBY: *(Brings out games pieces)* Let's start with boys versus girls. Sean, you play Kara. T. J., you play Jess. Alex, you play Stephanie.

The campers play their first round of games. JESS, KARA, and SEAN are the first-round winners.

JESS: *(Triumphantly to T. J.)* What do you say now, loser?

T. J.: *(With a sour expression)* You were just lucky, that's all.

JESS: Sounds like sour grapes to me!

ABBY: That's enough, you two. Jess, Kara, and Sean, come over to this table. Since Sean's the only guy left, we'll let him play in the next round against one of you girls. I'll flip a coin to see who plays him. Kara, call either heads or tails. *(Flips the quarter in the air)*

KARA: Heads.

ABBY: *(Catches the quarter in her palm and looks at it)* Heads it is! Kara, you play Sean. The winner will play Jess.

SEAN and KARA sit down to play. The other campers crowd around and watch. KARA quickly has possession of all of SEAN's checkers.

JESS: *(Takes SEAN's seat across from KARA)* Looks like it's you and me!

KARA and JESS play a game. JESS backs KARA into a corner.

KARA: How did you do this?

JESS: I told you, I learned from my grandma, the checker master.

KARA: You're too good for me, Jess. *(Uses her crutch to get up from her chair)* Looks like it's up to you, Abby!

ABBY: *(Sits down, and smiles at JESS)* Ready to get beat, Jess?

JESS: *(Strongly)* No way!

The other campers crowd around to watch. Abby and Jess play quickly. Soon each player has two kings and two checkers on the board.

STEPHANIE: Abby does everything well. I think she'll win.

KARA: Jess has some pretty smart moves though. Don't count her out.

Suddenly the lights go out. The room is very dark.

T. J.: Hey, what happened?

ABBY: *(Calmly)* The lights always go out when we've had a lot of rain. I know where there are some flashlights. Hang on.

ABBY leaves the table to get a flashlight. In the darkness, JESS adds another checker to the board. ABBY returns, glowing flashlight in hand.

ABBY: Well, now we can finish our game. *(Shining the flashlight on the checkerboard)* Whose move is it anyway?

JESS: I think it's your move, Abby.

ALEX: Wait a minute. How come you've got an extra checker, Jess?

JESS: What are you talking about? I don't have an extra checker.

T. J.: *(Studies the board)* Alex is right, Jess. Just before the lights went out you and Abby each had two kings and two checkers.

JESS: *(Defiantly)* So what are you saying? You think I'm a cheater?

ABBY: You must have just miscounted the checkers. Jess wouldn't cheat!

ABBY stares at the board, then moves one of her kings. JESS jumps all of ABBY's remaining checkers with the checker she added to the checkerboard.

T. J.: *(Patting JESS on the back)* Way to go, Jess!

ABBY: I better go to the mess hall and fire up the gas ovens. *(EXITS)*

As JESS puts away the checkers, the others congratulate her.

KARA: You play checkers well, Jess. Your grandma would be proud.

JESS: *(Mumbling)* I guess so. Look, my stomach's hurting. I think I'll go to bed. You guys enjoy the pizza. *(EXITS with head down)*

KARA: What's wrong with Jess? I thought she would be jumping for joy.

My *Life* in Jesus

What causes us to fall into temptation? Read the words of **1 Corinthians 10:12–13** from page 1. How are these words both a warning and a comfort? When you are tempted, what will God do for you?

The Lord will rescue me from every evil attack and will bring me safely to His heavenly kingdom.   *2 Timothy 4:18*

The Seventh Petition

But deliver us from evil.

What does this mean? We pray in this petition, in summary, that our Father in heaven would rescue us from every evil of body and soul, possessions and reputation, and finally, when our last hour comes, give us a blessed end, and graciously take us from this valley of sorrow to Himself in heaven.

What kind of prayer is the Seventh Petition?

The seventh petition is a summary petition in which we ask our Father in heaven to rescue us from the devil and all evil which has come into the world because of sin.

How does the Lord rescue us from every evil of body and soul, possessions and reputation?

In a world ruined by sin, the Lord keeps us from harm and helps us to endure the troubles that He allows to come into our lives.

What final deliverance from evil do we ask the Lord to bring to us?

We want our Father in heaven to keep us faithful to Him and when we die to take us from this sorrowful world to Himself in heaven.

Life Point

Through faith in Jesus, we confidently pray that God will rescue us from every evil and will someday take us to heaven to live with Him forever.

MY LIFE IN JESUS STUDENT LEAFLETS are published by Concordia Publishing House, 3558 S. Jefferson Ave., St. Louis, MO 63118-3968. Skit scripts written by Diane Grebing. Edited by Edward Grube. Scripture quotations: NIV®. Used by permission of Zondervan. All rights reserved. Catechism quotations: *Luther's Small Catechism with Explanation,* © 1986, 1991 CPH. Copyright © 2000 CPH. Printed in U.S.A.   22-2874

ABBY ENTERS the girls' cabin, shining a flashlight and holding a box of pizza. JESS lies on the bunk, pretending to be asleep.

Delivered

ABBY: (Cheerfully) Pizza delivery! Hot, fresh pepperoni pizza for the checker champ!

JESS: Go away! I'm trying to sleep.

ABBY: Since when do you go to bed at 9 P.M.? Are you feeling well? (Sets down the pizza and feels JESS's forehead) You don't feel hot.

JESS: Leave me alone, okay? I'm just not hungry.

ABBY: (Sits down on the edge of JESS's bunk) Why do I get the feeling that there's something else going on here? Kara and the others figured you'd be jumping for joy because you beat me. What's really going on?

JESS: (Quietly) I don't deserve any pizza because I didn't actually win the checker game.

ABBY: Of course you won. You jumped all my checkers on the last move.

JESS: The checker I used to win shouldn't have been there. While you were looking for the flashlight, I added it to the checkerboard.

ABBY: Why did you do that, Jess?

JESS: (Shrugs her shoulders) I don't know. I guess I wanted the others to like me. I figured if I won the game everybody would get pizza and I would be their hero. It seemed like a good plan at the time, until Kara said that my grandma would be proud of me. Then I just felt guilty. (Pauses) I wouldn't blame you if you hated me.

ABBY: I don't hate you, Jess. In fact, I forgive you.

JESS: Why would you do that for a cheater like me?

ABBY: We all make bad choices, Jess. The fact that you told me what you did shows that you know it wasn't right. Even if I had found out you cheated me, I would still forgive you.

JESS: (Sneering) That's the craziest thing I've ever heard!

ABBY: It may be crazy, but it's exactly what God does for every one of us. We all sin. We're all hopelessly lost in our sins on our own. We don't deserve God's forgiveness and mercy. But even though we don't deserve it, God loves us so much that He sent Jesus to deliver us from our sins.

JESS: *Deliver* us from our sins?

ABBY: That means He takes our sins away along with the punishment we deserve through Jesus' death on the cross. God rescues us from the eternal death and sorrow our sins cause. God also promises to deliver us from all evil and someday bring us to heaven, where we'll live with Him forever, eternally free from sin, pain, and sadness. (Grinning) That's some special delivery, huh?

JESS: (Smiling) It's even better than that pizza you brought in.

ABBY: (Holding up the plate of pizza) Hungry?

JESS: (Sits up in her bunk) Actually, I'm starved. Feeling guilty takes a lot out of you. (Looks down at the floor) Abby?

ABBY: What is it, Jess?

JESS: I'm really sorry I cheated.

ABBY: I thought we'd been through all this. I forgive you, Jess.

JESS: (Cautiously) I'd like to play you in checkers again, this time fair and square.

ABBY: I'd like that too, Jess. (Gestures at the pizza) You'd better eat up before it gets cold! (Pauses) Jess, there's something I need to tell you. I called your parents the other night. I invited them to our end-of-camp meal. They said they would like to come.

JESS: (Stares at ABBY) My parents make lots of promises that they don't keep. I'll believe they're coming when I actually see them here.

ABBY: I told them about the kindness you showed toward Alex at the lake and about how much I've enjoyed being your counselor.

JESS: After what I've told you tonight, I bet you wish you'd never said any of those things, right?

ABBY: No, Jess, I still mean every word. I'm anxious to meet your parents. I think we'll have a lot to talk about. I need to get back to the recreation center to lock up and make sure the others get back to their cabins by lights out. Enjoy the pizza. (EXITS)

JESS: (Thinking aloud) I've never met anyone like Abby. Even after all the rotten things I've done, she forgives me and still cares about me. Maybe there is hope for me and my parents …

My *Life* in Jesus

Why can you trust in God's forgiveness?

In a world full of evil, why can Christians have peaceful hearts?

Based on Jess's conversation with Abby, how does God's love change people's hearts?

The Conclusion

For Thine is the kingdom and the power and the glory forever and ever. Amen.

What does this mean? This means that I should be certain that these petitions are pleasing to our Father in heaven, and are heard by Him; for He Himself has commanded us to pray in this way and has promised to hear us. Amen, amen, which means "yes, yes, it shall be so."

Why do we end the Lord's Prayer with the word *amen?*

The word *amen* means "so shall it be" and emphasizes that God, who has commanded us to pray, will hear our prayers and answer them as He has promised.

How do I know God is able to answer the prayers of His people in Christ Jesus?

- He alone is the King who has all good gifts in His control.
- He alone has the power to grant our petitions.
- He has all glory and is worthy of our praise.

To Him who is able to do immeasurably more than all we ask ... be glory in the church and in Christ Jesus throughout all generations.
Ephesians 3:20–21

ABBY and THE CAMPERS stand at the base of a rock wall on the Camp Wonderment property. ABBY wears a climbing belt with several metal hooks. She carries a long, thick rope.

Life Point

When we pray, we can be sure God will hear and answer our prayers because He is our all-powerful Lord and King, who loves us and saves us through Christ Jesus.

Sure, I'm Sure!

ALEX: *(Looking upward)* Whoa! How high is it up to the top, Abby?

ABBY: I think about 50 feet. *(Pointing to the rock face)* This rock wall is actually pretty easy to climb.

STEPHANIE: Easy for you, maybe. I'm kind of afraid of heights.

ABBY: You don't have to climb it, Stephanie. Lots of campers don't like to do it. But when you reach the top, the view's pretty cool.

T. J.: How do you get up to the top without falling?

ABBY: If you decide to climb it, I'll hook you up with ropes so in case your foot slips, you won't fall back to the ground. I'll also climb right beside you. If you start to slip a little, I can steady you.

ALEX: Are you sure it's safe?

ABBY: Sure, I'm sure. I've taken 50 campers up to the top before.

KARA: Well, I know I'm out of this activity because of my knee.

ABBY: I'm afraid that's true, Kara, but if you come back next year, you can try it then. I do have an important job for you, though.

KARA: Sure thing! What do want me to do?

ABBY: *(Takes her camera out of her pocket)* I'd like you to take some pictures of us as we climb. *(Moves over next to KARA)* Just push this button here when you're ready to take a picture.

KARA: Looks easy. I'll be happy to do it.

ABBY: Great! Now, who's ready to go first?

SEAN: *(Hesitates)* If it's okay with you, Abby, I think I'll just stay here next to Kara. She might need some help with the camera.

ABBY: That's fine, Sean. You don't have to climb if you don't want to.

STEPHANIE: That sounds like a good plan, Sean. Mind if I stand and watch with you and Kara?

ALEX: I'll join you guys. I've had enough excitement here in the lake. I don't need a rock-climbing disaster to add to my camp scrapbook.

KARA, SEAN, STEPHANIE, and ALEX stand together and watch ABBY, T. J., and JESS.

ABBY: Well, it looks like it's the three of us.

T. J.: *(Stuttering)* I … I … I guess so, Abby. You're sure this is safe?

ABBY: *(Reassuringly)* Sure, I'm sure, T. J. You're far too important to me. I won't let anything happen to you. Would you like to go first?

T. J.: All right. At least if I fall it will be while I'm doing something adventurous.

ABBY: Let's get you hooked up. *(Hooks a belt on T. J. and attaches a rope to it and to her own belt)* You're all set. Come with me.

ABBY and T. J. walk to the bottom of the rock face. While the other campers watch, ABBY shows T. J. the path they'll take to scale the face. T. J. nods in understanding. Slowly they climb up the face together, quickly reaching the top.

SEAN: *(Calling upward)* Hey, T. J.! How's the view?

T. J.: *(Looking around)* Neat! I can see the whole camp from up here.

ABBY unhooks T. J. from her belt and rappels back down to the ground.

ABBY: *(Looking at JESS)* Your turn, Jess.

JESS: My stomach feels like it's full of butterflies. Will I be okay?

ABBY: Sure, you will. That's just your nerves talking to you. T. J. did great. I know you will too.

ABBY hooks JESS up with a belt and rope and gives JESS the same instructions she gave T. J. They begin to climb as KARA, SEAN, STEPHANIE, and ALEX watch. About halfway up the rock face, JESS's right foot slips.

STEPHANIE: Oh, no, Jess is slipping!

ABBY immediately steadies Jess and helps her replace her foot on a rock ledge. They climb to the top.

KARA: *(Calling upward)* Are you okay, Jess?

JESS: *(Smiling triumphantly)* I'm great! *(Looking at ABBY admiringly)*

ABBY: *(Waving down to KARA, SEAN, STEPHANIE, and ALEX)* Hey, Kara! Get our picture up here.

ABBY, JESS, and T. J. pose as KARA shoots the photo.

ABBY: *(Calling down)* We'll take a hiking path down the other side of the hill and meet you guys at the craft cabin, okay?

ALEX: *(Shading his eyes and calling up to ABBY)* Are we going to make those camp shirts you talked about when we first came here?

ABBY gives ALEX the "thumbs up" sign.

ALEX: I've got some great ideas! C'mon, guys, let's go! *(ALL EXIT)*

My *Life* in Jesus

What makes for a trusting relationship between two people?

In what ways did Abby's actions toward T. J. and Jess mirror God's actions toward you?

How can you be sure God will hear and answer your prayers?

What is Baptism?

Baptism is not just plain water, but it is the water included in God's command and combined with God's word.

Which is that word of God?

"Therefore go and make disciples of all nations, baptizing them in the name of the Father and of the Son and of the Holy Spirit" (Matthew 28:19).

What great and precious things are given in Baptism?

Baptism

- works forgiveness of sins;
- rescues from death and the devil;
- gives eternal salvation.

If Christ has already won forgiveness and salvation for us and gives us all this by grace alone, why do we still need Baptism?

Christ has indeed won full forgiveness and salvation for the whole human race with His perfect life, suffering, death, and resurrection. He distributes this same forgiveness in Baptism. (Baptism is a means of grace.)

To whom does Baptism give all these blessings?

Baptism gives these blessings to all who believe God's saving promises.

Life Point

In Baptism, God cleanses us from our sins, clothes us in Christ, and gives us new identities as His children.

MY LIFE IN JESUS STUDENT LEAFLETS are published by Concordia Publishing House, 3558 S. Jefferson Ave., St. Louis, MO 63118-3968. Skit scripts written by Diane Grebing. Edited by Edward Grube. Scripture quotations: NIV®. Used by permission of Zondervan. All rights reserved. Catechism quotations: *Luther's Small Catechism with Explanation,* © 1986, 1991 CPH. Copyright © 2000 CPH. Printed in U.S.A.

22-2874

All of you who were baptized into Christ have clothed yourselves with Christ. *Galatians 3:27*

ABBY and THE CAMPERS sit at a large work table inside the craft cabin. Behind them hang a number of T-shirts with logos designed by campers from the other cabins.

New Clothes

STEPHANIE: Boy, these shirts are pretty neat. Do you see that one from cabin 10 that says "We're Perfect 10s!"?

KARA: That's clever. I like these from cabin 8. *(Points upward)* They used pine cones and leaves like stencils to make designs. Even though everyone used the same materials, each shirt came out different.

JESS: I wonder what our shirts will look like?

ALEX: *(Excitedly)* I've had this great idea ever since we first came here to camp. I think our shirt should have a logo on it. Each of us could think of something for each part of it. That way all of us would have our own part, yet it would stand for all of us together.

T. J.: Hey, I like that idea!

SEAN: I do too, but I'm not very good at drawing.

ALEX: *(Encouragingly)* That's okay, Sean. I'll help you draw it.

STEPHANIE: So how do we know what to put on our individual parts?

ALEX: I thought that maybe each of us could draw a picture or use words to describe our favorite or most memorable part of Camp Wonderment. I think that our finished logo would make a pretty good picture of all the different things about this camp.

ABBY: That's a wonderful idea, Alex! What shape should we use?

KARA: Definitely a circle. It's round so everybody could have an equal part to work on.

STEPHANIE: And a circle is equal all the way around and never ending. It shows how we're united together here at camp.

JESS, T. J., and SEAN nod in agreement.

ALEX: Then a circle it is! *(Gets a piece of paper and a pencil from the shelf. Draws a large circle on the paper.)* This should do it. *(Holds up the paper and shows the group)* Including Abby, there are seven of us. I'll mark the circle into seven equal parts and cut them off the paper. Then I'll hand out a part to everyone and you can sketch your ideas.

ALEX mark, cuts, and distributes the paper sections. THE CAMPERS and ABBY busily draw and write. After a short time, KARA speaks.

KARA: I'm done!

SEAN: Me too.

ABBY: How about the rest of you?

T.J., JESS, STEPHANIE, and ALEX put down their pencils and hold up their papers.

ALEX: Okay. *(Showing his paper)* This is probably no big surprise to you, but I drew the lake. After all, it's where I had my big adventure.

ALL laugh.

STEPHANIE: That's neat, Alex. Mine's about my big camp adventure too. *(Showing her paper to the group)* See, it's the snake on the nature hike. I drew a slash through it to remind me how Abby protected me.

T. J.: I remember that! Here's mine. *(Showing his paper to the others)* It's the rock we climbed. It was so neat to get to the top and look all around.

SEAN: *(Holding up his paper)* Mine might be hard to figure out. *(Pointing)* Here's my yo-yo in the middle. This hand here is mine and the other belongs to Alex. See how the hands touch? At first we had a problem about the yo-yo, but Abby helped us work it out. The hands are supposed to be shaking, showing we're forgiven friends.

KARA: That's a good drawing, Sean. *(Showing her paper)* My picture is of Grandpappy Oak. When I saw this tree on our nature hike, I was amazed. It reminds me of the awesome things God has created.

JESS: *(Holding up her paper)* Mine's pretty simple. It's a heart with a cross on it. *(Looking around at everyone)* You've all been kind to me, even when I haven't been the same way toward you.

ABBY: I am so impressed with everyone's drawings! They're wonderful!

T. J.: C'mon, Abby. Let's see yours.

ABBY: All right. *(Showing her paper)* My drawing has six smiling faces on it, one for each of you. Each one of you is so special to me.

ALEX: These drawings are going to make a great logo! I can't wait until they're all put together. Abby, where are the silk-screening supplies?

ABBY: I'll get them for you, Alex. *(EXITS)*

ALEX: Now comes the fun part! If we work quickly, we can print the shirts and wear them to chapel tomorrow!

My *Life* in Jesus

According to **Galatians 3:27** (page 1), what "new clothes" do all baptized people have?

What blessings does God give us at Baptism? (See page 4.)

The campers selected these symbols for their camp shirts—water, snake with "no" sign, rock, shaking hands, a tree, heart with cross, and smiling faces. What might these symbols have to do with your life in Jesus?

The Power of Baptism: *How can water do such great things?* Certainly not just water, but the word of God in and with the water does these things, along with the faith which trusts this word of God in the water. For without God's word the water is plain water and no Baptism. But with the word of God it is a Baptism, that is, a life-giving water, rich in grace, and a washing of the new birth in the Holy Spirit.

What Baptism Indicates: *What does such baptizing with water indicate?*

It indicates that the Old Adam in us should by daily contrition and repentance be drowned and die with all sins and evil desires, and that a new man should daily emerge and arise to live before God in righteousness and purity forever.

What is the Old Adam? The Old Adam is the corrupt and evil nature that we inherit because of Adam's fall into sin.

How is this Old Adam to be drowned in us? The Old Adam is to be drowned by daily contrition (sorrow for sins) and repentance (faith), by which we resist and overcome evil desires.

What is the new man? The new man is the new spiritual life and nature, created in us by the washing of rebirth.

How is this new man to emerge and arise? The new man emerges and arises as we daily live and grow before God in true faith and good works.

How does Baptism indicate the daily drowning of the Old Adam and the emergence of the new man? By Baptism we have been made to share in Christ's death and resurrection. As He has buried our sin, so we too can and must daily overcome and bury it. And as He is risen from the dead and lives, so we too can and must daily live a new life in Him.

Life Point

In Baptism, we are given new, eternal lives and the power to serve God and others.

MY LIFE IN JESUS STUDENT LEAFLETS are published by Concordia Publishing House, 3558 S. Jefferson Ave., St. Louis, MO 63118-3968. Skit scripts written by Diane Grebing. Edited by Edward Grube. Scripture quotations: NIV®. Used by permission of Zondervan. All rights reserved. Catechism quotations: *Luther's Small Catechism with Explanation,* © 1986, 1991 CPH. Copyright © 2000 CPH. Printed in U.S.A.   22-2874

If anyone is in Christ, he is a new creation; the old has gone, the new has come! *2 Corinthians 5:17*

ABBY and THE CAMPERS stand around the altar in the Camp Wonderment chapel at the end of the chapel service.

New Hearts

SEAN: It was really neat seeing everyone in their new shirts during chapel today.

T. J.: There were all those different cabin groups, yet everyone was there as one large group to worship Jesus.

ABBY: There are more new things here today than just shirts.

STEPHANIE: What do you mean? I don't see anything new added inside the chapel.

ALEX: We couldn't have gotten any new campers, because this camp session's almost over.

ABBY: The new things I'm talking about aren't so easy to see, unless you know what to look for. And actually, some of the new things are invisible.

JESS: Is this some kind of riddle?

ABBY: (Chuckling) Oh, Jess, I don't mean to sound so mysterious. You have a lot to do with the new things I'm talking about.

JESS: (Looks herself over, then shrugs her shoulders) Hey, Kara, do you notice anything new about me?

KARA: (Smiling) Yes, I do, Jess. You're acting like a new person. And I think I know why. (Looks at ABBY) Jess has a new heart, doesn't she, Abby?

ABBY: You're right, Kara. But Jess isn't the only one with a new heart. We've all got one. Every day, God renews the promises He made through His Word when we were baptized. He promises to forgive our sins, strengthen us, help us grow in His Word, and give us power to serve Him and others. All His promises are connected through this … (Points at cross)

T. J.: The cross? I know that Jesus died on the cross for our sins, but how are God's promises to us connected to it?

ABBY: Our Baptism connects us to Christ's cross in several ways. In a way that no human being can fully understand, all of our old sinful selves hung with Jesus on the cross. Through Baptism, our sinful nature died with Jesus. Then we were raised with Jesus to live a new life. The Holy Spirit is at work constantly in our hearts. The more the Holy Spirit helps us understand our cross connection, the

more of His power we have. All during our time together at camp, I've seen this power at work in each one of you.

SEAN: How?

ABBY: I see it in the ways that you show God's love and forgiveness toward each other. I see it in the ways that you help and encourage each other. I see it in the ways that you've grown to trust God and to come to Him in prayer when you need help. Actually, it's like I have a whole new group of campers since you first came here.

THE CAMPERS look at one another and grin.

T. J.: Then maybe we should reintroduce ourselves! Hi! I'm T. J. I'm a new creation in Christ!

ABBY: (Laughs and holds out her hand in greeting to T. J.) It's nice to meet you, T. J.! I'm Abby. God makes me new too!

ALL take turns reintroducing themselves to one another as new creations in Jesus.

JESS: Attention, everyone! This new person wants to pray!

ALL join hands around the altar and bow their heads.

JESS: Heavenly Father, thank You for making me a new person in Jesus. Thank You for making us Your sons and daughters through faith. Help all of us use the power You give us in Baptism to daily love You and others. In Jesus' name I pray. Amen.

ALEX: "Yes, yes, it shall be so!" Right, Jess?

JESS: Right, Alex!

My Life in Jesus

Based on what Abby shared with the campers, what is new about you ?

What are some relationships in your life right now where you can see God's power in Baptism at work?

What are some relationships in your life right now where you could better share and show God's love? Ask the Holy Spirit to help you with these relationships.

If we confess our sins, He is faithful and just and will forgive us our sins and purify us from all unrighteousness. *1 John 1:9*

What is confession?

Confession has two parts.

First we confess our sins, and second, that we receive absolution, that is, forgiveness, from the pastor as from God Himself, not doubting, but firmly believing that by it our sins are forgiven before God in heaven.

What sins should we confess?

Before God we should plead guilty of all sins, even those we are not aware of, as we do in the Lord's Prayer; but before the pastor we should confess only those sins which we know and feel in our hearts.

Which are these?

Consider your place in life according to the Ten Commandments: Are you a father, mother, son, daughter, husband, wife, or worker? Have you been disobedient, unfaithful, or lazy? Have you been hot-tempered, rude, or quarrelsome? Have you hurt someone by your words or deeds? Have you stolen, been negligent, wasted anything, or done any harm?

Life Point

God leads us to admit our sins to Him and to others, and He forgives our sins for Jesus' sake.

MY LIFE IN JESUS STUDENT LEAFLETS are published by Concordia Publishing House, 3558 S. Jefferson Ave., St. Louis, MO 63118-3968. Skit scripts written by Diane Grebing. Edited by Edward Grube. Scripture quotations: NIV®. Used by permission of Zondervan. All rights reserved. Catechism quotations: *Luther's Small Catechism with Explanation,* © 1986, 1991 CPH. Copyright © 2000 CPH. Printed in U.S.A.

22-2874

JESS, STEPHANIE, and KARA stretch out their sleeping bags and fluff up their pillows on their cabin bunks. They talk to each other before lights out.

A True Confession

STEPHANIE: *(Yawning)* Wow, am I ever tired! It was a lot of work getting the mess hall ready for tomorrow's end-of-camp meal.

KARA: It's hard to believe that tomorrow is the last day of camp. The time's gone by really fast.

STEPHANIE: No kidding! But I am excited about getting home and seeing my parents and my friends. I sure have a lot to tell them!

KARA: Me too! When I called my mom the other day, I told her all about the shirts we made. She's excited to see what they look like. *(Looks over at JESS)* Hey, Jess, you're pretty quiet. Aren't you excited about going home?

JESS: Not really.

STEPHANIE: I know you've had some rough times with your mom and dad, but aren't you getting tired of sleeping in these hard bunks. *(Punches the mattress)* I can't wait to get home to my own bed.

JESS: *(Quietly)* If I tell you guys something, will you promise not to laugh?

KARA: Of course.

JESS: Stephanie?

STEPHANIE: I promise too. This sounds pretty serious. *(Climbs up on the edge of JESS's bunk)*

JESS: I don't want camp to end because I'm scared to see my parents.

STEPHANIE: You're scared? You? You always seem so tough.

KARA: *(Kindly)* How come you're scared, Jess?

JESS: Do you remember those notes we sent home the first week?

KARA: I remember. We were supposed to let our parents know how things were going and tell them what we liked about camp.

JESS: Well, in my note I told my parents that what I liked about camp was that I didn't have to be at home with them.

STEPHANIE: You really wrote that?

JESS: Yeah. Pretty stupid, huh?

KARA: We all say things that we don't mean, Jess. I'm sure your mom and dad would understand if you just explained it.

JESS: That's just the point. I don't know how to explain it. At the time I wrote the note, I was really mad that they sent me off to camp. But camp's turned out to be a really good place. The more I've been around Abby and all of you, the more I've realized that being angry

and saying hurtful things is no solution to any problem. But I'm really afraid that my parents are so upset about what I wrote that they'll never forgive me and that things will never be right between us.

ABBY ENTERS.

ABBY: What will never be right, Jess?

JESS: *(Suddenly quiet)* Oh, nothing.

STEPHANIE: *(Nudges JESS)* It's okay. Tell Abby. I'm sure she can help.

JESS: I'm scared that after all I've said to my parents they won't want me to come home with them. I realize now that what I said really hurt them. I hurt inside too. I don't know how to make things right.

ABBY: God's already taken the first step to bring you and your parents back together, Jess. He's helped you realize that your words and actions were not the best ways to act. God helped you to feel sorry about what you've done.

JESS: But that doesn't make it any easier to tell my *parents* that I'm sorry. I know God forgives me, but what if my mom and dad won't?

ABBY: God doesn't just work in your heart, Jess. He'll work in your parents' hearts too. God will be right there with you when you talk to them. It's not easy to say you're sorry. But God promises to help. You know, Jess, God says that if we confess our sins, He is faithful and just and will forgive our sins and clean our hearts. You can be certain that God's forgiven you for Jesus' sake. You can also be certain that He will help you confess your sins to your parents. Would it help if I was with you tomorrow when you talk to them?

JESS: Would you, Abby? It would make me feel so much better.

ABBY: I'll be there, Jess. *(Looks at her watch)* Wow, it's 11 o'clock, way after lights out. We've got a busy day tomorrow. We'd better hit the sack. *(Turns out the lights in the cabin)*

JESS: Thanks, Stephanie, Kara, and Abby for talking with me.

STEPHANIE: You don't have to thank us, Jess. We're friends.

My *Life* in Jesus

Based on what Jess said as she talked to Abby, Stephanie, and Kara, what does true confession involve?

Read **1 John 1:9** from page 1. How are these words a comfort when we are led to recognize our sins?

How can depending on God and His forgiveness help when you need to confess a sin to someone you have wronged?

Confess your sins to each other and pray for each other so that you may be healed.
James 5:16

The Office of the Keys

What is the Office of the Keys?

The Office of the Keys is that special authority which Christ has given to His church on earth to forgive the sins of repentant sinners, but to withhold forgiveness from the unrepentant as long as they do not repent.

Where is this written?

This is what St. John the Evangelist writes in chapter twenty: The Lord Jesus breathed on His disciples and said, "Receive the Holy Spirit. If you forgive anyone his sins, they are forgiven; if you do not forgive them, they are not forgiven." [John 20:22–23]

What do you believe according to these words?

I believe that when the called ministers of Christ deal with us by His divine command, in particular when they exclude openly unrepentant sinners from the Christian congregation and absolve those who repent of their sins and want to do better, this is just as valid and certain, even in heaven, as if Christ our dear Lord dealt with us Himself.

Life Point

Jesus gives to the pastors of His church the authority to forgive sins in His name and encourages us to share the Good News of forgiveness in Him with others.

MY LIFE IN JESUS STUDENT LEAFLETS are published by Concordia Publishing House, 3558 S. Jefferson Ave., St. Louis, MO 63118-3968. Skit scripts written by Diane Grebing. Edited by Edward Grube. Scripture quotations: NIV®. Used by permission of Zondervan. All rights reserved. Catechism quotations: *Luther's Small Catechism with Explanation,* © 1986, 1991 CPH. Copyright © 2000 CPH. Printed in U.S.A.

22-2874

THE CAMPERS and ABBY are busy in the mess hall setting the tables for the end-of-camp meal.

The Reunion

ALEX: There sure is enough stuff to do to get ready for a meal! I thought, after all the work we did yesterday, we could take it easy today.

ABBY: (Chuckling) This should give you a newfound appreciation for all that your parents do for you at home.

T. J.: Maybe so, but they don't have to set the table for over 100 people!

STEPHANIE: (Finishes setting the name cards at each place setting) Hey, Abby! How does this look?

ABBY: (Looking over at STEPHANIE) It looks wonderful, Stephanie. All of you have been working really hard.

DENNIS and JEAN (JESS's parents) ENTER. They stand in the doorway.

ABBY wipes her hands and goes over to Dennis and Jean.

ABBY: Welcome to Camp Wonderment! (Extends her right hand in greeting) I'm Abby, one of the counselors here.

DENNIS: (Shakes ABBY's hand) I'm, Dennis. This is my wife, Jean.

ABBY: Hello, Jean. It's good to meet you. I'm so glad you're here.

JEAN: It's a pleasure to meet you too. We spoke over the phone a few days ago. (Scans the room anxiously) Is Jess here?

ABBY: Yes, she's back in the kitchen with Kara and Sean, helping the cooks clean some vegetables for the salad. Let me go and find her.

ABBY EXITS. After a pause, ABBY and JESS ENTER.

JESS: (Nervously) Hi, Mom. Hi, Dad. (Looks down at the floor and then back at her parents' faces) I see you found the camp.

JEAN: (Awkwardly hugs JESS) We've missed you, Jess.

JESS: (Surprised) You have?

JEAN: Well, of course we have! (Stands back and looks at JESS) I know it's only been two weeks, but it seems to me you've grown a little taller.

ABBY: (Smiling) It's funny, isn't it, how different someone can look, even after a short time. Actually I think you'll find several other things about Jess that are different too. Why don't we go outside and talk?

JESS gives ABBY a pained look. JESS, DENNIS, and JEAN follow ABBY outside the mess hall and walk along the main path through the camp. They stop and sit on two benches along the path.

JESS: How's Cody?

JEAN: He's fine, Jess. I think he missed having his sister around to bug.

JESS: (Gives a small grin, then looks down and speaks quietly) I've missed you guys too. I … I've got something I need to tell you. I'm really sorry about the things I said to you in my note and on the phone.

DENNIS: Jess, we don't understand why you're so upset with us. When your mom and I signed you up for camp, we thought you'd enjoy being away from home for a while, making new friends.

JESS: I have enjoyed those things. But I thought you and Mom sent me here because you didn't want me around the house.

JEAN: Jess, we love you. We didn't do this to send you away from us.

JESS: Abby and the other campers were so kind, even though I took a lot of things out on them. They helped me see that saying angry words isn't the right way to act toward anyone, especially my parents. After I said and wrote all those mean things, I was afraid you would never forgive me. I can't blame you if you don't.

DENNIS: Jess, we do forgive you. Your words did hurt your mother and me at first. That's why we mentioned that maybe you would be happier if you went to stay with your grandparents.

JEAN: We have something to say to you, too, Jess. I know you think that your dad and I haven't spent much time with you lately. I confess that sometimes we've spent too much time working. Please forgive us. We'll try to do better. As a matter of fact, we've got some things planned to do with you and your brother over the rest of the summer.

ABBY: That sounds pretty neat, don't you think, Jess?

JESS: (With a broad smile) Oh, yes! (Gives JEAN and DENNIS a big hug, then looks upward) Thanks, God.

ABBY: God's worked in all our hearts, hasn't He, Jess?

JESS: Oh, yes, Abby, just like He promises to! Abby, would you say a prayer with my mom and dad and me?

My Life in Jesus

How is the process of confession at work in the story?

Tell about a time you experienced the same relief and forgiveness after confessing your sin to someone.

The words of **James 5:16** on page 1 talk about the healing God gives when He forgives (absolves) our sins. Healing occurs as well when we forgive others and they forgive us.

How do you see this at work in Jess and her parents? in your own life?

What is the Sacrament of the Altar?

It is the true body and blood of our Lord Jesus Christ under the bread and wine, instituted by Christ Himself for us Christians to eat and to drink.

Where is this written?

The holy Evangelists Matthew, Mark, Luke, and St. Paul write:

Our Lord Jesus Christ, on the night when He was betrayed, took bread, and when He had given thanks, He broke it and gave it to the disciples and said: "Take, eat; this is My body, which is given for you. This do in remembrance of Me."

In the same way also He took the cup after supper, and when He had given thanks, He gave it to them, saying, "Drink of it, all of you; this cup is the new testament, in My blood, which is shed for you for the forgiveness of sins. This do, as often as you drink it, in remembrance of Me."

What is the benefit of this eating and drinking?

These words, "Given and shed for you for the forgiveness of sins," show us that in the Sacrament forgiveness of sins, life, and salvation are given us through these words. For where there is forgiveness of sins, there is also life and salvation.

Life Point

The Lord's Supper is a means of grace where God offers, gives, and seals forgiveness of sins, gives us strength to love Him and our neighbor, assures us that we are one with Christ and other believers, and comforts us with the hope and joy of eternal life.

My Life in Jesus Student Leaflets are published by Concordia Publishing House, 3558 S. Jefferson Ave., St. Louis, MO 63118-3968. Skit scripts written by Diane Grebing. Edited by Edward Grube. Scripture quotations: NIV®. Used by permission of Zondervan. All rights reserved. Catechism quotations: *Luther's Small Catechism with Explanation*, © 1986, 1991 CPH. Copyright © 2000 CPH. Printed in U.S.A.

22-2874

Whenever you eat this bread and drink this cup, you proclaim the Lord's death until He comes. *1 Corinthians 11:26*

THE CAMPERS sit at a table in the mess hall. T. J. and KARA sit next to each other, as do ALEX and JESS. These four campers are on one side of the table. SEAN, and STEPHANIE sit across from them on the other side of the table. They are enjoying the end-of-camp meal.

A Very Special Meal

ABBY stands at the head of the table with a box.

ABBY: *(In a loud voice)* It's a tradition at Camp Wonderment for the counselors to give their campers a special blessing at the end-of-camp meal. I've enjoyed being with these six young people over the past two weeks. I think we've really grown together as friends in Christ. I am going to miss them a lot when camp is over. *(Opens up the box)* Would Alex please come up here with me for a moment?

ALEX gets up from the table and stands next to ABBY.

ABBY: Alex, my blessing for you is from Daniel 6:27: "[God] rescues and He saves." *(Pulls a bottle of water out of the box)* Alex probably provided the most excitement during this session with his little incident in the lake. So, Alex, here's a bottle of lake water so that you will always remember your rescue here and God's rescue through the water of Baptism.

ALEX: *(Holding up the bottle of water for all to see)* Thanks for coming to my rescue, Abby. I'll never forget what happened!

ALL cheer as ALEX sits down.

ABBY: Stephanie, you're next!

STEPHANIE rises to stand by ABBY. ABBY pulls a stick out of the box.

ABBY: Can you guess what this is for?

STEPHANIE: Does it have to do with that snake on the nature trail?

ABBY: *(Smiling)* That's right! Stephanie, my blessing for you is from Psalm 23:4: "Even though I walk through the valley of the shadow of death, I will fear no evil, for You are with me, Your rod and Your staff, they comfort me." Remember, that Jesus is always guiding and protecting you.

STEPHANIE: *(Holding up the stick)* I hope I won't ever have to use this on another snake!

ALL cheer as STEPHANIE sits down.

ABBY: *(Takes plaster-cast handprint out of box)* Sean, please come up here.

SEAN gets up from the table and stands next to ABBY.

ABBY: Your yo-yo tricks astounded us, Sean. But even more astounding was how helpful you were to all of us. You have a servant's heart! My blessing to you is "The Lord is my helper; I will not be afraid," Hebrews 13:6. *(Presents the plaster hand to SEAN)* I made this cast of my hand over in the craft cabin. Whenever you look at it, remember how much I appreciated all your help.

SEAN: *(Hugs ABBY, then takes the plaster hand and shows it to the others)* I had the best time of my life here, Abby. Thanks for everything.

As SEAN is seated, ALL cheer. ABBY takes the rock out of her box.

ABBY: Come on up, T. J. It's your turn.

T. J. walks up and stands near ABBY.

ABBY: I was very proud of you and Jess the day you climbed the rock wall. *(Hands T. J. the rock)* Here's my blessing to you from Psalm 18:2: "God is my rock, in whom I take refuge."

T. J.: Climbing that rock was one of the neatest things I've ever done. Thanks for helping me, Abby.

ALL cheer as T. J. sits down.

ABBY: *(Pulls a leather key chain out of the box and goes to stand next to KARA)* Despite an injured knee and walking with a crutch, Kara went everywhere and never complained about anything. *(Gives KARA the leather foot)* Here's a foot-shaped key chain I cut from leather that will help you remember my blessing for you, "[God] will not let your foot slip—He who watches over you will not slumber," Psalm 121:3.

KARA: Thanks for being so understanding about my knee, Abby. Even though I didn't get to do everything, I had a great time here.

ALL cheer for KARA as ABBY walks back to the head of the table.

ABBY: My last award and blessing goes to Jess. Come on up here with me.

JESS walks to the head of the table and stands next to ABBY.

ABBY: *(Puts a heart-shaped necklace around JESS's neck)* God has changed your heart since you arrived at camp. I know that the Lord will continue to work in your heart. My blessing for you is from Matthew 22:37: "Jesus replied: 'Love the Lord your God with all your heart and with all your soul and with all your mind.' "

JESS: Oh, Abby. Thanks for all your patience with me.

ALL cheer as JESS returns to her seat.

My *Life* in Jesus

Abby gave some special blessings to the campers as they ate their end-of-camp meal. Carefully read the catechism text about the Lord's Supper from page 4. What blessings does God give to all people through this special meal?

The Power of the Sacrament of the Altar

How can bodily eating and drinking do such great things?

Certainly not just eating and drinking do these things, but the words written here: "Given and shed for you for the forgiveness of sins." These words, along with the bodily eating and drinking, are the main thing in the Sacrament. Whoever believes these words has exactly what they say: "forgiveness of sins."

Who receives this sacrament worthily?

Fasting and bodily preparation are certainly fine outward training. But that person is truly worthy and well prepared who has faith in these words: "Given and shed for you for the forgiveness of sins."

But anyone who does not believe these words or doubts them is unworthy and unprepared, for the words "for you" require all hearts to believe.

[Jesus said,] "I am the vine; you are the branches. If a man remains in Me and I in him, he will bear much fruit; apart from Me you can do nothing." *John 15:5*

Life Point

As we receive the Lord's Supper with repentant hearts, we remember Jesus' sacrifice as He graciously forgives our sins and gives us eternal life.

MY LIFE IN JESUS STUDENT LEAFLETS are published by Concordia Publishing House, 3558 S. Jefferson Ave., St. Louis, MO 63118-3968. Skit scripts written by Diane Grebing. Edited by Edward Grube. Scripture quotations: NIV®. Used by permission of Zondervan. All rights reserved. Catechism quotations: *Luther's Small Catechism with Explanation,* © 1986, 1991 CPH. Copyright © 2000 CPH. Printed in U.S.A.

22-2874

THE CAMPERS are busy hauling their gear to the front of the camp as they get ready to go home. ABBY watches as THE CAMPERS work.

Remember ME

SEAN: (*Wiping his brow*) This is hard work! How come it seems like we've got so much more gear now than when we first got here?

T. J.: (*Lumbering by SEAN with a load of belongings*) I don't know. Maybe it's because dirty laundry weighs more than the clean stuff.

ALEX: (*Handing SEAN his yo-yo*) Hey, Sean, I really did find this on the floor under the bunk this time.

SEAN: (*Gratefully*) Thanks, Alex. I wouldn't want to leave this behind.

STEPHANIE: (*Groaning under the weight of her bags*) Whoa! Remind me next year not to bring so much stuff.

JESS: (*Grinning as she carries a small backpack and sleeping bag*) I'll help you pack for next year. You need to travel light, like me!

KARA: (*Hobbles out using her crutch, as her backpack hangs from her shoulder*) I'll get the rest of my stuff when my mom gets here. (*Turns to JESS and STEPHANIE*) Did I hear you two say you're coming to camp next year?

JESS: I wouldn't miss it! Hey, we need to sign up to be roommates in the same cabin again. Don't forget to put that on your applications, okay?

STEPHANIE and KARA nod yes. ABBY walks up with a camera.

ABBY: Has everyone got everything packed?

T. J.: Our cabin's spotless, Abby. There's not a cheese doodle in sight!

ABBY: (*Laughs*) Good job, T. J. I know the camp maintenance people will appreciate your cleanliness, even though the ants won't!
I want to get a group picture so I won't forget what you look like. (*Looks around*) How about if everyone stands under the camp sign?

THE CAMPERS assemble under the sign. ABBY takes their picture.

ABBY: Now I've got one more thing I need each one of you to do for me. (*Takes out a small notebook*) I need each of you to sign this notebook with your name and address so I can drop you a note from time to time. (*Thumbs through the pages*) I didn't realize how full the pages of my book were getting. Let's see . . . this page should do.

ALEX: Wow, Abby, are those all the campers you've ever been a counselor for?

ABBY: Yes, Alex, plus all the names of all the people whom I ever bunked with at Camp Wonderment when I was a camper like you.

KARA: That's sure a lot of names to remember. How do you keep everyone straight?

ABBY: I try to remember people by something special they did or by some special quality they had. (*Pulls a pencil out of her pocket and hands KARA the book*) Here, Kara. Why don't you start?

One by one, THE CAMPERS write their names and addresses into ABBY's book. At last, JESS hands it back to her.

T. J.: (*Steps forward holding an envelope*) This is for you, Abby, from all of us. But you have to promise not to open it until we've left, okay?

ABBY: But why can't I open it now?

SEAN: You'll understand when you open it. (*Turns around suddenly*) Here's my grandpa. (*Gives ABBY a quick hug*) See you again, Abby. Have a great summer. (*Picks up his gear and turns back to the other campers*) Later, guys. (*Turns and EXITS*)

THE OTHER CAMPERS look around and notice that their families are ready to leave too. As THE CAMPERS pick up their stuff, they give ABBY a hug, say good-bye, and then EXIT. JESS is the last one to leave.

JESS: I'll never forget you, Abby. Thanks for everything you did for me.

ABBY: I wasn't the only one who helped you, Jess.

JESS: (*Smiling*) Oh, I know. I've been thanking God at least five times every day for all He's done! I've got to go. I know I'll see you again. (*EXITS*)

ABBY: (*Eagerly opens the envelope*) Oh, my! (*Looks at the cover of the card and reads aloud*) To Abby, who helped show us Jesus. (*Opens the card*) Thank you for all you have done as our counselor and friend. We will never forget you, and if we don't see you again at camp, we know we'll see you in heaven! Love, Alex, Sean, T. J., Kara, Stephanie, and Jess. (*Holds the card to her heart and bows her head*) Heavenly Father, thank You for letting me get to know these young people. Strengthen their faith and love for You. In Jesus' name I pray. Amen.

My *Life* in Jesus

What are some things you do to remember Jesus and all that He does for you?

What do you think is the most important truth that we need to remember about Jesus?

How does Holy Communion remind Christians of this most important truth?

Read **John 15:5** from page 1. Why is it so important that we stay close to Jesus throughout our entire life?